Mexican
Days

Mexican
Days

Journeys into the Heart of Mexico

Tony Cohan

Broadway Books
New York

BROADWAY

MEXICAN DAYS. Copyright © 2006 by Tony Cohan. All rights reserved. No part of this book may be reproduced or transmitted in any form or by any means, electronic or mechanical, including photocopying, recording, or by any information storage and retrieval system, without written permission from the publisher. For information, address Broadway Books, a division of Random House, Inc.

Note to the Reader: In an effort to disguise the identities of several individuals, the author has changed their names and in some cases disguised identifying characteristics or used composite characters.

Grateful acknowledgment is made to Sacha Newly for permission to quote from his description of his visit to Hacienda Katanchel.

Every reasonable effort has been made to obtain permission for copyrighted material included in this work. Any errors that may have occurred are inadvertent and will be corrected in subsequent editions, provided notification is sent to the publisher.

PRINTED IN THE UNITED STATES OF AMERICA

BROADWAY BOOKS and its logo, a letter B bisected on the diagonal, are trademarks of Random House, Inc.

Visit our Web site at www.broadwaybooks.com

Book design by Donna Sinisgalli
Map by Jackie Aher

Library of Congress Cataloging-in-Publication Data
Cohan, Tony.
    Mexican days : journeys into the heart of Mexico / Tony Cohan.
      p. cm.
    1. Mexico—Description and travel. 2. Cohan, Tony—
Travel—Mexico. I. Title.
    F1216.5.C65 2006
    917.2—dc22

                                    2005052705

ISBN-13: 978-0-7679-2090-2
ISBN-10: 0-7679-2090-2

10 9 8 7 6 5 4 3 2 1

First edition

For Karen Margrethe

Contents

I.

1. Once Upon a Time in Mexico   3

2. La Gruta   17

3. Surreal in the Sierra Gorda   29

4. Dreamers and Mad Monks   47

5. City of Mud   63

6. Toledo's Ghost   79

7. Techno Tribal   91

8. Dinner with Lauren   103

9. Fitzcarraldo and Dr. Leroy   125

10. La Frontera   143

II.

11. The Yellow House   151

12. The Gringo Jarocho   163

13. Katanchel: Sacha's Honeymoon   181

14. To Palenque   199

15. Conversations with Pakal   215

16. Fridamania   229

17. Restless Fiesta   243

III.

18. Fugue   263

"What is travel and what use is it? One sunset is much like another; you don't have to go to Constantinople in order to see one."

FERNANDO PESSOA, *THE BOOK OF DISQUIET*

"Man needs escape as he needs food and deep sleep."

W. H. AUDEN

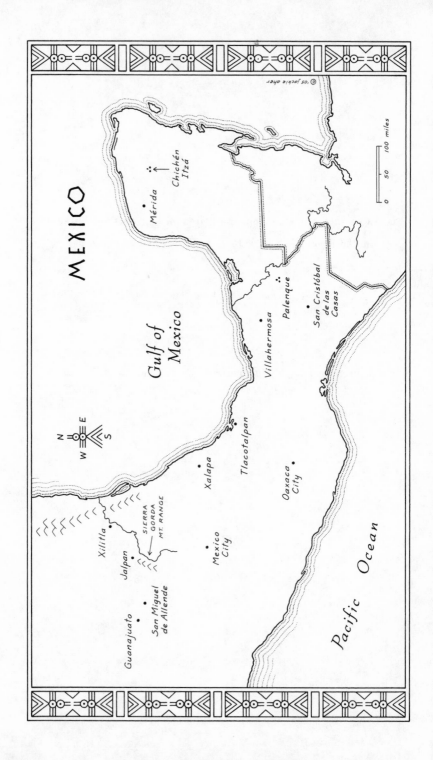

One

"Where does a trip begin? Where does the first idea come from?
But then, where does a love, a friendship, begin?"

—PAUL MORAND, *VOYAGE TO MEXICO*

1.

Once Upon a Time in Mexico

So what do you make of this?" said Xavier.

I watched, from behind a cordon of yellow police tape, Antonio Banderas in a mariachi outfit, and Salma Hayek in far less, dangling from cables affixed to the rooftop of the Hotel San Francisco in San Miguel de Allende's central plaza, *el jardín*. Walkie-talkies crackled in Spanish and English. A utility van edged slowly past with a card taped to its windshield reading ONCE UPON A TIME IN MEXICO.

"*¡Acción!*"

A volley of fake gunshots burst forth; cameras droned. As the pair descended on the cables in the burnished early twilight, kicking the air, I realized they weren't Antonio and Salma at all but stunt doubles. "Cut!" I heard in English. Then I saw, over the heads of the gawkers, the real Johnny Depp, pale and slight, emerging from Xavier's dad's restaurant with his lady, Vanessa Paradis, on his arm. Willem Dafoe swung into view, followed by Cheech Marin. Was that Mickey Rourke across the plaza? Rubén Blades? Girls' screams signaled the arrival of the true Banderas, Melanie Griffith close beside him; then *la* Salma herself with her swain, Edward Norton.

Cast and crew had been shooting for months in and around San Miguel, Xavier said. Local nerves were frayed. First flutters of pride and curiosity had given way to resentment. Shopkeepers were up in arms at street blockades preventing access to their stores. An old gringo had cursed out a camera crew some days earlier, to the amusement of the local town paper, *Atención*—as if he had any more or less right to be here than they did. Hungry locals, hoping to hire on for a few days' work as extras in a bullfight scene, complained about low pay and dry sandwiches. News had leaked out that Melanie Griffith refused to leave the room while a woman masseuse attended to Antonio.

"They've rented our town," Xavier said. "Or maybe I should say they've bought it."

Banderas and director Robert Rodriguez, of *El Mariachi* fame, hoping to mollify criticism for "not giving something back to the community," were going to show *Spy Kids* for free in the plaza that night for the benefit of local youth. The massive movie screen had been installed in front of the Museo Ignacio Allende, obscuring the statue of San Miguel's native son and revolutionary hero, and folding metal chairs were stacked against the old wall across from the Parroquia, the parish church. Banderas would speak to the kids beforehand, thank the community, and introduce the film.

It was a late summer afternoon, the town walls flaring brick red as the sun tipped the mountains across the Guanajuato Plain—golden time for the cameras, no doubt. Over and over the couple dropped like spiders from the Hotel San Francisco roof, accompanied by flurries of gunshots.

"They've been shooting the same scene for three days," Xavier said bleakly.

I'd been away for a while, doing necessary things, all the while dreaming of sweet return. I suppose I should have been amused at the irony: former refugee from the movie capital of the world finds himself tripping over cable wires, kliegs, and booms trying to get back to his house in this once-remote old town in the central Mexican highlands. But it had been a tough trip: two weeks earlier, the attacks on the World Trade Center and the Pentagon. Leaving LAX for Mexico that morning had been like passing through an armed camp. This was hardly the soft landing I'd imagined on the flight down.

We slipped away from the flower sellers, bullhorns, and stargazers crowding the *portales* around the plaza and headed down Calle Umarán. Passing a gaggle of tourists in front of Restaurant La Mama, Xavier said ruefully, "If I see another Frida Kahlo tote bag, I'm getting out my gun."

Laughing, we came to my street, where we exchanged an *abrazo* and agreed to meet up later.

Ducking under police tape, I bore my luggage down Calle Flor in the soft, spreading twilight. This had been a favored foot route from the old Hotel Ambos Mundos, where I stayed when I first came here, to the shady bowers of the Parque Juárez: then the steep climb beyond to El Chorro, the beautiful old waterworks and site of the town's founding in 1521 by the friar San Miguel. Calle Flor, a three-block ribbon of rough cobbles sloping southwest from the town center, retained a mix of large and small homes behind its high, lime-washed walls. Not the fanciest street in town, but a pretty one, and if it showed up in an occasional postcard, video, or Mexican soap opera, this was only fitting tribute.

As the commotion of the jardín receded, I glimpsed beyond the curving descent a swatch of enameled sky, darkening blue to ebony, crosshatched with black grackles and white egrets winging their way home. Above the hill's rim, where the road called El Caracol twists down into the town, steely cumuli gathered for their quick, violent nightly assault, cleansing the cobbles and cooling the summer evening before ceding the sky to starlight. The once-barren hillside had filled in with homes over the years, the tangle of electrical wires obstructing its view now buried underground (a public fiasco in which the manhole covers kept caving in, sending unwary pedestrians to the Hospital de la Fe with broken legs or worse).

When I first knew Calle Flor, there were few shops or restaurants along it. Now the first block hosted a bookstore, an art gallery, two popular café-restaurants, a hair salon, a realty office, a home furnishing shop, two jewelers' boutiques, and a house-techno pulque bar late at night. The next block, where we lived, remained residential but for an old jeweler who kept sketchy hours and a neighborhood *tiendita* run by a family who sold soft drinks and small provisions; and where an Italian restaurant had flowered one long-ago summer and we danced the nights away to salsa bands, a dry cleaner emitted steam into the street.

Our immediate Mexican neighbors—Dr. Ramírez and his family to our left, the retired Sánchezes to our right—remained in place. Rogelio the painter across the street still rented rooms to young women he hoped would pose nude for him. Timoteo, maestro carpenter of wooden religious statues, maintained his permanent window display of a manacled Jesus in purple velveteen robe and still fashioned his extraordinary crèches every year for the Night of the Altars during Holy Week. And Diego, town scion and environmentalist, kept his organic garden and beautiful grove of trees intact in the big house across from ours.

Reaching my door, I fished out the key, turned it in the lock, and stepped inside. My luggage slumped to the *entrada* floor. The tall mesquite door closed behind me with its deep, consoling thunk.

I exhaled into the silence.

That evening, after a thundershower, I left the house and walked several blocks to El Petit Bar on Calle Hernández Macias. Founded by a couple of old acquaintances, Jacques and Sophie, "Le Petit," as it was called, had become a watering hole of choice the last few years, reflecting the town's new cosmopolitanism. Jacques's quirky, sculpted furniture and lighting, the subdued speaker throb of Brian Eno or St. Germain or Leonard Cohen, offered an alternative to the Andean flutists, mariachis, and cool jazz found elsewhere around town. Deeper inside the old property they'd lived in years ago, when they were still married, a courtyard restaurant gave play to Sophie's art and cuisine.

Jacques and Sophie had migrated to San Miguel the year we did, after living for some years in the Peruvian Amazon. He French, she French-Canadian, architects by trade, they'd raised their two towheaded boys here before sending them off to Havana, one to become a keyboardist, the other to study with the Cuban National Circus. At El Petit Bar regulars mingled with newcomers, local news circulated, and romances bloomed or died. You could look at the art on the walls, read Jacques's trilingual monthly culture magazine, *El Petit Journal*, or simply sip in silence watching people. Here Jacques, genial host, seemed to have found his true métier.

I located Xavier in a deep leather chair, drinking tequila in the company of a young woman he introduced as Lluisa from Barcelona, here visiting a friend on the movie set. Xavier, wry poet and relentless anatomist of the town, was a tender misanthrope, a cheerful fatalist. Hopelessly romantic, he dreamed of the world beyond while showing little interest in actually visiting it. He pursued women, and sometimes men, with the same wishful languor. Once a month he taught a writing class at the local prison above the town, and on Sundays he ran a poetry workshop at Bellas Artes Institute. He tilted at a pre-Columbian/postapocalyptic epic verse novel he'd probably never finish. He knew English—I'd caught him once in the jardín reading *The New York Review of Books*—but steadfastly refused to admit it, remaining comfortably embedded in Castil-

ian, inviting you to come over and meet him there. Droll di-
agnostician of chance, he considered himself a disciple of the
Guatemalan writer Augusto Monterroso, perhaps best known
for having written the shortest short story in the world: *"Cuando
despertó, el dinosaurio estaba todavía ahí."* (When he awoke, the
dinosaur was still there.)

By way of catching me up, and no doubt to amuse the
fetching Lluisa, Xavier began briefing me on local develop-
ments in my absence. A woman we'd known, an avid flyer
and proprietress of a notoriously overpriced restaurant, had
allegedly embezzled money from her sister-in-law, an aged
writer, then inexplicably crashed her Cessna into a mountainside in coastal Oaxaca. A kidnapper known as the Earlopper
was running amok in nearby Querétaro. Xavier really warmed
to news of Epifánio, a contractor around town who'd helped me
build the stairs to my roof. It seems Epifánio had started up a
cantina and whorehouse outside of town—prostitution is legal
in the next state over but not in this one—and now was in the
hospital with broken legs and ribs after leaving the cantina at
five-thirty in the morning with four of his prostitutes, then
crashing his car into a village chapel trying to outrun police.
More poetically, and dearer to us, a shy, beautiful girl named
Paloma who sold books at the Bellas Artes and had never ut-
tered a word had suddenly, mysteriously burst into speech.

A boisterous gang from the movie crew piled into the bar,
and soon we couldn't hear ourselves think, let alone speak.
Xavier proposed we move on to La Cucaracha on Calle Zacateros, living descendant of the old bar where Kerouac and

Cassidy had guzzled in the 1950s. But still feeling the effects of the day's travel, I took this as my cue to say an early goodnight.

The oft-repeated tale of origins that San Miguel de Allende tells itself—scrolling past as if depicted on a mural, left to right, divided into three large, vivid-hued panels—begins with a mythic past of Chichimeca and Otomi Indians living close to the earth until a kindly Franciscan father arrives to enlighten them; then enters history as the colonial epic unfolds literally inside San Miguel homes, where a heroic priest and a colonel conspire to overthrow the Spanish Crown; then climaxes as modern travelers discover that the little mountain town, four hours north of Mexico City, is a paradise. San Miguel de Allende: site of fiestas and miracles, ecstatic religion and fiery revolt, unearthly beauty and curative air—a place for dreamers and artists.

Its truer history—less symmetrical, less seemly, grislier—records that the *indígenas* were enslaved or driven off, the few surviving descendants sometimes still to be found in tattered costumes selling dolls along the first block of Calle Flor. Father Hidalgo's and Colonel Allende's heads dangled in cages for ten years on the granary wall of nearby Guanajuato after they were hunted down by the Spanish, the end result of their revolt being to establish a new aristocracy of local landowners, requiring another, bloodier revolution later that delivered equally dubious results. The old weed-clotted town cemetery next to the church of San Juan de Dios, now so oversubscribed its locked metal gates forbid entry, brims with the earthly remains of victims of deadly epidemics that ravaged the town. As for the Inquisitor's House on Calle Pila Seca, it would rather keep its ghosts safely hidden away behind the antique furniture now sold there.

Set in an agrarian region with wealth derived from the nearby silver mines of Guanajuato, San Miguel long served as a traders' and travelers' stopover. In centuries past it functioned as the region's slaughterhouse, and Calle Flor was a street of tanners. In the late 1700s residences came to be built, including sections of this abandoned, decaying structure we'd bought in 1988 for very little. After the Revolution of 1910 and the violent Catholic counterrevolt that followed, the town fell into a kind of slumber, the old colonial houses sinking into decay, the fiestas desultory, the churches and monasteries languishing. Tunnels that ran beneath the town, and our house, collapsed, though rumors of buried treasure still circulate. A train running between Mexico City to the Texas border sometimes stopped at the foot of San Miguel to take on water, collect mail, and discharge or admit the occasional passenger.

An educated Peruvian vagabond named Felipe Cossío del Pomar debarked from that train in the late 1930s, became enchanted by the place, and founded an art institute on the grounds of a sprawling hacienda that belonged to a leading family of the town. A gentle, resourceful, eccentric American, Stirling Dickenson, arrived around the same time, as did José Mojica, a Mexican opera star who built a rambling home bordering Juárez Park. A massive, deserted nunnery in the town center became another art school. When soon after World

War II some young Americans came to study art on the GI Bill and *Life* magazine wrote it up—"How to Live in Paradise for $100 a Month"—the third panel of the mural was begun. Still quiet, beautiful, and cheap when Kerouac, Cassidy, Ginsberg, and Burroughs passed through, scattering legend in their wake, San Miguel gradually gained currency among artists, backpackers, and a handful of foreign retirees. More years passed, and journalists began writing up this "hidden gem" in the travel magazines. When a new airport nearby shortened the trip here by half, tour agencies started working it into their packages.

In the coda, or epilogue, of the narrative—the fourth panel of the mural, sketched in but unfinished, hidden in a shaded alcove in its ambivalence or shame—burros become automobiles, the old ruined facades sleek hotels and bars, the stone buttress of the parish church the site of a pricey restaurant, the town square thronged with T-shirted tourists. In this depiction, old-timers and locals are seen fleeing in the face of the desecrations. This panel, like the David Álfaro Siqueiros mural in San Miguel's Bellas Artes building, may forever remain unfinished. Entitled, perhaps, *Tarnished Eden*, it bears no more or less proximity to truth than the other panels. After all, if the idea of a traveler's paradise is a cliché, so is its ruination.

I'd always thought San Miguel, steeped in 450 years of custom and tradition, its population still over nine-tenths Mexican, would, like many an Italian hill town, remain safely inured from the worst effects of all this. Tourists and foreign residents occupied a parallel world for the most part, and a few blocks' stroll away from the central plaza sharply reduced their numbers, to the null point as one reached the outskirts. Many North Americans didn't seem to particularly notice the people in whose midst they lived any more than they did back home, unless they performed a service for them. Seen from the other side, gringos, for all our exaggerated self-regard, were, in the end, but a blip on the Mexican screen.

Arriving in the middle of filming that day, I wasn't so sure.

Back at the house, not yet ready to sleep, I climbed the stone stairs to the roof and groped my way to the veranda Epifánio and I had built some years back. Propping my feet against the edge of a table hewn from an old hacienda door, I let my eyes slowly adjust to the profusion of starlight that always seems so close overhead in these mile-high mountains. An early moon hung like a scythe over Atascadero Hill. Across the scramble of rooftops, the lit sandcastle spires of the Parroquia church appeared near enough to reach out and touch. A bat that lived in the *entrada* emitted his sonar blip. Insects rustled the air.

For sixteen years San Miguel de Allende's winding lanes, patios, and church bells had offered sweet respite to a couple of "refugees from the techno-future," as I'd once described us. After living first in a hotel, then in a small rented house, Masako and I had come upon this deserted ruin and, to our amazement, bought it. I'd never been inclined to identify myself by where I hung my hat, but inside these yard-thick walls we'd marked the turning years, proof against the folly of the world beyond and our own vagaries. Here we'd lived through earthquakes, fires, floods, and fiestas; deaths, births, romances, and separations of friends. Behind these walls, blessings less easily measured—magic, silence, *alegría, corazón*—had come to us.

The last few years, without consciously deciding it, we'd found ourselves spending more time away—from this house, from each other. There was always some reason: tangled in work webs of our own making, dealing with family matters back in the States. This time it had been a trip to California to see to my father's final affairs; he'd passed away the fall before, ending a lengthy senescence. Then writing work had taken me to Southeast Asia for a month. Masako was in southern Mexico completing a book on Mexican textiles, to be published the following year. When we did meet up these days, we weren't quite sure what to do next, how to get back in sync. As always in our long marriage, the instinct was to let it be, to allow time, and time apart, to sort it out, bring us back together. Separate journeys, often with an excuse, sometimes not even bothering with one: testing our connection to each other, to the life we'd made here in Mexico. Lately even friends had begun to notice we were seldom here, or any place, at the same time. This house on Calle Flor, metaphor of renewal, sometimes lay empty.

We accrete histories even in the places we flee to. Empty white rooms fill up with things. Dreams become accomplishments stacked behind like firewood or abandoned like scrap. As San Miguel de Allende morphed from sleepy secret to popular tourist site, merging into its image of itself, becoming a postcard—a video, a feature film—filling with people we'd once left behind, would all we'd discovered, named, and built together here hold? Now suddenly downtown New York City was a steaming crater. My country was finding new enemies, readying for war. The earth was moving under all our feet.

I looked down into the rear garden, a cluster of dark shapes by starlight. I used to sit on that old stone bench built into the back wall and steal a smoke, when I smoked. My secret garden wasn't so secret now: the señora next door had sold the back plot off to her sister, whose new *casa de huéspedes*, bed and breakfast, towered above our ancient garden wall, blocking the sun.

I'd always sensed my hold on existence here to be conditional. Life in a poor country like Mexico was ever tenuous at best, all arrangements provisional, even if the governor of our state had been elected president of the country on a platform of reforms the country still awaited. Still, like the *golondrinas*, the swallows who return to breed in the entrada, I always came back, *con gusto*. And there was always a moment in the day, week, or season when the street returned to its inhabitants, this house remained the heart's abode, and all seemed the way it was, once upon a time in Mexico.

The Parroquia lights dimmed, died. Across the patio a light came on in the kitchen of our *casita* where a writer friend was staying for a few months. Smiling, I took the stairs down from the roof.

In the bedroom I noticed a blinking light on the answering machine. Among messages I hadn't checked when I'd arrived was one from the editor of a travel magazine in New York, wondering if I'd be interested in taking some trips around Mexico—visit other regions and towns, see how the puzzle of old and new fit together, write about it.

I lay in bed in the dark, pondering this sudden *invitation au voyage*.

2.

La Gruta

The next morning I awoke to blessed silence. Dreams of lost luggage, a stolen passport, an incomplete list diffused into the high beamed recesses of the ceiling. I gazed blearily at my still-packed suitcases on the bedroom floor. Out the tall window, first sunlight tipped the pergola of the casita. An iridescent hummingbird sipped from a fat orange blossom of the trumpet vine trailing down the patio wall. The deep bell known as La Luz tolled its muffled call to matins at La Parroquia.

I was back. And all I'd loved I still loved.

A volley of small explosions erupted: firecrackers announcing a neighborhood fiesta, that rowdy dawn custom so familiar to San Miguel residents and irritating to visitors. The loud cracks stopped, then began again, in patterned salvos.

No, it wasn't firecrackers but gunshots. Filming was starting early at the Hotel San Francisco.

Struggling up, I went to the kitchen and found just enough

Chiapas coffee left to make a strong cup. Another fusillade of bullets burst forth from the jardín.

I washed, slipped into some clothes, and headed out, thinking I'd mull over the writing proposal at breakfast somewhere in the *centro*. Stepping out onto Calle Flor, I saw a crowd of extras, dressed as tattered Mexican peasants, surging toward me, urged on by bullhorns, trailed by cameras on dollies. Cornered like a *borracho* at San Miguel's yearly September *pamplonada*, the bull run, I ducked back inside just ahead of their charge and slammed the door.

I went to the phone and called the editor back.

Later that morning, when the film crew had moved on to their next setup, I left the house. Avoiding the jardín, which still resonated with gunshots, I walked down Pila Seca and flagged a taxi.

"La Gruta," I said to the driver, climbing in beside him.

We bumped down Calle Canal, a street encoded with ghost recollections of fiestas and parades, *moles* and *mariscos*, walks taken alone or with friends—textures laid into memory like the coats of lime wash on these old colored walls. The medieval enclosure of the colonial center widened to reveal a glistening strip of lake at the foot of town, *la presa*, swollen with water from months of summer rains.

The *taxista* turned north at the two-lane road toward the town of Dolores Hidalgo. Quickly we left behind old San Miguel on its hill, racing past sections of "new" town that grew ceaselessly outward these days in rings—new *colonias*, little un-surfaced brick neighborhoods with their own names. Soon we hit open *campo*, windows down, fresh morning air buffeting the cab.

I'd never had a car in Mexico. Once I tried to figure the costs of owning one compared to hopping taxis and buses, or renting an occasional car, and decided I'd come out ahead. But the calculation had less to do with economics than with what be-ing here meant: a respite from California driving for a life on foot, open to encounters, pauses, the mysteries hidden in slow-ness. In Mexico I took the stance of a pilgrim, inviting correc-tives to the limitations of the culture I came from, revelations offered me here as boons.

Twenty minutes outside San Miguel, the taxi let me off at a small crossroads beside a low running wall with the hand-painted words LA GRUTA. Across from it, a whitewashed sign with an arrow said ATOTONILCO. The taxi sped off, leaving me alone in the empty morning. Tiny insects buzzed about my head. A black crow cawed from the twisted limb of a *pirule* tree.

The groundwater around the nearby village and penitent shrine of Atotonilco is uniformly hot (in fact the word *atotonilco* in Nahuatl means "place of hot waters") and feeds the baths of La Gruta, "The Grotto." On full moon nights La Gruta hosted hedonistic gatherings of San Miguel New Agers, and on week-ends tourists took over, but I hoped that on this quiet morning it would be mine alone.

I slipped through the gate onto the untended property. Passing a large swimming pool drained of water, I came to a fence bordering a stream where Chichimecan women scrubbed clothes on rocks. I parted a cluster of tall cane in the middle of the field and stood before a small blue oval pool filled with clear water. Hidden from the gaze of the giggling washerwomen, I slipped out of my clothes, lowered myself over the edge, and sank in. Swimming the length underwater, I came up dripping at the other end. I dangled at the edge, panting, my chin on my arms, listening to a church bell, a tardy cock's crow, a car accelerating on the highway beyond, my mind filling, then emptying, with all it had taken to get here.

A big spring issue, focusing on Mexico, the editor had said. *What's interesting these days? Take some trips. Look around the country. Not the usual treatment . . .*

The prospect excited me, of course. I found Mexico endlessly alluring. It had been a long while since I'd traveled around; with the years, as I'd settled into San Miguel, inevitably I'd journeyed less to other regions. An article could help finance a trip to South America I'd had in mind. But I'd just set my bags down in San Miguel after a round of travels, barely tasted arrival. And it was hard to think straight with Robert Rodriguez and crew shooting up the town.

I clambered out of the pool, wrapped a towel around me, and walked through an opening in a stone wall to a paved area with old rusty lockers. Leaving my clothes in one, I lowered myself into an open rectangular pool surrounded by banks of palms, cacti, and flowers. I swam to the far end, where steaming groundwater coursed from a narrow arched tunnel, and waded into the chest-high current. Sliding onto my stomach, I paddled up ascending locks in darkness toward distant dancing beams of light. Rough stone walls brushed my skin; the rising roar of water filled my ears.

I came to a domed brick chamber: the grotto. Shafts of light from pinholes in the roof made little rainbows in the steam. A waterfall surged from an opening high in the dome. Slithering over the rim into the circular pool, I stroked toward the hot, deafening cascade and stood beneath it, eyes closed, shoulders drooped, letting the torrent blast my thoughts to smithereens.

Several months before, in an airport waiting room in the Vietnamese town of Hue, I'd come upon a discarded, week-old copy of *The New York Times*. In it I'd read a review of the new edition of *The Merck Manual of Medical Information*. It described a curious disorder called "dissociative fugue," in which "one or more episodes of sudden, unexpected and purposeful travel from home (fugue) occur, during which a person cannot remember some or all of his past life." I'd been struck enough by the article to cut it out and stick it in my notebook.

Over the last few years a spate of wanderings had picked up a momentum I couldn't seem to arrest. I only felt comfortable while in motion, it seemed. Sitting at a window seat as a plane lifted off a tarmac in Bangkok, Vienna, or Newark had a soothing effect that no amount of channel surfing or pumping iron could rival. Gazing across a Macedonian lake to Armenia on the far shore; staring into the thatched recesses of a Buddhist monastery ceiling in the Burmese hills; standing at Denmark's northernmost tip watching the currents of two seas collide;

driving too late and too fast at midnight down Big Sur's Highway 1—all these brought strange solace. If each journey had its raison d'être—writing work as often as not, or family matters—few had been truly unavoidable had I not wanted to go. Displacement as steady state; escape as arrival; flight as sanctuary.

Half seriously, half in jest, I'd considered the possibility that I'd fallen prey to some form of this disorder I'd read about in the airport in Hue. Certainly the wanderings that had beset me were often "sudden, unexpected and purposeful," in Merck's terms. Unlike the condition described, I seemed to have no difficulty remembering some or all of my past life; in fact, I seemed to remember more than I cared to. But then how can we know what it is we don't recall? I didn't mind thinking of my recent travels as a "fugue," with its evocation of Bach's divine inventions—*fugue* meaning, of course, "flight." But the word also carried another definition: "a disturbed state of consciousness."

The condition has a high incidence, apparently: two people in one thousand in the United States are affected by dissociative fugue, according to Merck. "A person in a fugue state usually disappears from his usual haunts . . ." "Often the person has no symptoms or is only mildly confused during the fugue . . ." "During the fugue, the person may appear normal and attract no attention . . ."

Shades of Hitchcock and Cary Grant, or a Patricia Highsmith novel: a madman on a train, calmly reading a newspaper. It sounded a little romantic, even.

Though often mistaken for malingering, Merck says, because it may enable someone to avoid an unwanted circumstance, dissociative fugue is not faked. Rather, "many fugues seem to represent a disguised wish fulfillment . . .

"Most fugues," says the *Merck Manual*, "disappear on their own."

The waterfall's incessant pounding brought me back into myself. I slid away and floated in the dim waters.

Not the usual treatment. Take your time. Start where you are. Find it, don't design it . . .

The editor had been standing at her downtown office window, where a few weeks earlier the World Trade Center towers had impeded her line of sight across the East River. What would travel mean now, in the light of this change? Impossible to say. Mexico and Latin America seemed out of the line of fire for the moment, possibly a preferred tourist destination—hence her interest in a piece?

Strange, how yesterday everything was shaped by arrival; now suddenly things appeared in the light of departure. If I were truly in the grip of some manner of fugue, this *invitation au voyage* was teasing me back out into another episode.

I'd told her I'd call her back later that afternoon.

Where to begin a piece on Mexico? There was nothing monolithic about the country except its great temples and pyramids. Few countries offered more diversity in food, dress, customs, culture, landscape—from Caribbean to Pacific coasts, mountains to desert to jungle, modern cities to ancient villages. Beneath a thin patina of chain stores and cybercafés, a layered culture stretched back twenty thousand years, maybe more. A new president and party were in power, broaching fresh realities even Mexicans had yet to understand. Mexico City had swelled to nearly twenty million people. I wouldn't recognize Oaxaca these days, Masako had said. A filmmaker friend would be shooting new archaeological breakthroughs at ancient Mayan sites in southern Mexico in the spring and had invited me to join him. Meanwhile San Miguel was occupied by a cadre of foreign troops dispatched by Hollywood, and the greater world convulsed toward unreadable confrontations.

I slithered out of the grotto and back down the tunnel on my stomach. In the warm open pool, I bobbed like jetsam—sun-blasted, limbs limp, mindless—until I heard approaching voices over the walls.

Still in a kind of reverie from the baths, I took a narrow, unpaved road leading away from the highway. My body, trunks, and towel dried quickly in the sun. New *huaraches* cut my feet. Crossing a stone bridge shaded by pepper trees, I walked alongside a high adobe wall bordering a pig farm. Snortings and stench bit the air.

I came into a wide clearing of crumbling arches and shuttered doors. The massive facade of the holy sanctuary of Atotonilco loomed in the dust and silence. The plaza was deserted but for two makeshift wooden stalls—one selling soft drinks, the other whips the *penitentes* used to flay their backs.

If modern Mexican history began here, I suppose mine did too. Paul and Mina, two friends who had come to Mexico decades earlier, had first brought me to this mysterious site. Paul, an artist of surreal tastes who would die too soon, had reveled in its hallucinatory extravagance, and my occasional revisits to Atotonilco always seemed fitting homage to him.

Even the word *Atotonilco* sounded strange, otherworldly, as if spoken in a dream, evoking some lost civilization—a dark, robed people with enlarged cerebrums worshiping alien deities. Squinting into the sun, I tried to discern in the weathered facade traces of the swirling murals and mystical inscriptions that time had etched away. I could just make out a shadow of an angel figure, a lone blurred Jesus.

A hunched nun was opening the great doors to the interior. I crossed the stony forecourt and followed her inside. Everything darkened; then as my eyes adjusted, a delirium of fantastical visions emerged. The wooden entry doors swarmed with panels depicting lurid scenes from the Last Judgment—a bestiary of horrors and raptures, entwined with mystical poems and inscriptions, sonnets and quatrains: "Gentle Lamb, thou showest me / By cruel lashes torn / Thy wounded back, which I / Most humbly venerate." The whole effect, images and texts, brought to mind *Songs of Innocence and Experience*—but Atotonilco was built fifty years before William Blake's book of poems was published.

In the cool, dim interior, hectic frescoes and fervid inscriptions covered the walls and vaults. Dolorous virgins, eyes cast heavenward, swooned in piety and adoration. Illuminated serpents and insects devoured men. Wooden saints dripped with *milagros*, junk silver charms. Florid religious paintings hung in peeling gold-leaf frames above twisted sculptures of saints. In chapels feeding off the nave, Venetian mirrors refracted musty light.

In a chapel off the altar, I heard chanting and moaning behind the walls. Through a keyhole I glimpsed penitents in sackcloth walking in a circle, flaying each other's backs, trailed by a cleric intoning a dirge.

Atotonilco was said to be many things: the birthplace of "the first Mexicans," where Father Hidalgo launched the revolt against the Spaniards in the name of the Virgin of Guadalupe; a holy shrine for pilgrims who come to purify their sins through rites of flagellation; and Mexico's earliest and largest repository of native American pictorial art, or *arte popular*. But it was the outrageous aestheticism, and the palpable sense of mystery, that always amazed me. If, on a whim, Jorge Luis Borges had invented an imaginary shrine in collaboration with Hieronymus Bosch and Dante Alighieri, it might have come out something like this.

Begun in 1740, Atotonilco was built over twenty-three years by two god-intoxicated men—a Spanish priest, Luis Felipe Neri de Alfaro, and a native artist, Miguel Antonio Martinez de Pocasangre. The mines of nearby Guanajuato were producing much of the world's silver then, and in reaction to the excesses unleashed by this vast wealth, and the increasing secularization of churches, holy communities sprang up devoted to spiritual exercises of penitence and punishment. Alfaro and Pocasangre had intended a shrine of purification and renunciation; when in fact they created a site of aesthetic excess and self-mortification far more orgiastic than the decadence they'd sought to counter. In spite of later additions and alterations, it was the copious, ecstatic art of Pocasangre, and Alfaro's charged, mystical poems (signed "San Juan de la Cruz"), that still dominated the sanctuary.

I wended my way back through the chapel as if swimming up from the depths of a watery dream. Nearing the entrance, I heard voices outside, some sort of commotion. Xavier had mentioned the night before at El Petit Bar that the movie crew had been scouting locations around Atotonilco—the old Spaniards had, after all, left spectacular movie sets wherever they built. Steeling myself for another collision with the gang from *Once Upon a Time in Mexico*, I stepped warily out into the bleached light of the square.

What I saw wasn't Salma or Antonio, Dafoe or Depp, but Mexican reality: a procession of tired, dusty, poor pilgrims who had come here from afar on foot. Paying me no notice, they filed past into the sanctuary chapel, singing in unison, their eyes shining with piety and adoration.

Back at the highway, I flagged a passing Coca-Cola truck. We rode to town in the dry midday heat, jiggling with the sounds of empty bottles, San Miguel's hilltop spires rising ahead of us. The flutter of excitement, the familiar contours of the road. Traces of what I'd just experienced at Atotonilco and La Gruta.

Yes, it felt like the beginning of a trip.

———

That night I sat on a favorite bench in San Miguel's jardín, next to the little pergola bandstand, where the Sunday evening concerts shook the air and rousted the birds from the Indian laurels. I watched a band of Japanese tourists with digital cameras shooting La Parroquia with all the absorption of surgeons, listened to oversize gringos in Bermuda shorts lacing the air with English, observed a wealthy Mexico City couple jabbing at cell phones while their teen slacker kids idled nearby doing the same. Inwardly I winced, wishing there were fewer of them, or they'd behave better, or just clear out and leave us alone.

Turistas, I thought, with all the ingrained snobbism of the long-term *residente* who'd arrived in an earlier, better time, a gilded era unreadable to these parvenus, interlopers, latecomers—not yet realizing that I was about to become a *turista* again myself.

3.

Surreal in the Sierra Gorda

I shouldn't have entered the jungle that late. It was already near twilight, and there was a light rain. I was stiff and tired from driving since dawn, and you can't always gauge time well in the jungle's permanent shade. But I wanted to at least get a glimpse of what I'd come far to see.

Passing the steep turnoff to the town of Xilitla, I crossed a small bridge, turned at a roadside *refresco* stand, and bumped the rented VW over mud, stone, and gravel. Humid forest closed in around me. Coming in view of a tall, decorated iron gate flanked by cement columns shaped like clusters of bamboo, I pulled over and turned off the engine.

I paid eight pesos, about eighty cents, to a quiet man in a sombrero sitting beneath a *palapa* just inside the gate. He didn't have change for my twenty-peso note. I told him to keep it—it was a matter of about a dollar—but he insisted on going to find *cambio* and disappeared. Enveloped in the cool shadows of the jungle floor, waiting for the honorable *caballero* to return, I began to notice sounds—squawking birds, whirring insects, a running stream somewhere below. Odd, barely discernible structures peeked through dense foliage on the sloping mountain above me.

I'd let many years in Mexico pass before coming to Las Pozas. A surrealist "art park" built by a wealthy English eccentric in this remote Huasteca region of the Sierra Gorda, far above the Gulf Coast, wasn't high on my list of Mexican must-sees. From what I'd heard, Edward James's unfinished fantasy had fallen into disrepair and disuse since his death in 1984. The idea of a rich man pouring millions into a personal art *folie* didn't seem all that indulgent in an era of athletes' ballooning salaries, instant Internet billionaires, and obscene payouts to corporate bosses. But I expected to be disappointed.

In truth, it was another mad builder of the Sierra Gorda who held equal interest to me, enough for me to finally undertake the twisting, vertiginous six-hour journey from San Miguel into these high tropical mountains. Two hundred years before Edward James, a Mallorcan mystic and monk had come here to build his first five missions in the Americas—I'd spent part of the day visiting three of them—before moving north to construct nineteen much larger, simpler ones, becoming a figure every Californian knows and a nominee for sainthood: the Franciscan brother Junípero Serra. So these two unusual men, one an aesthete, one a friar, had found expression in this distant corner of Mexico.

Edward James, poetaster and art patron, had been a genuine figure in modernist art milieus—collaborator and collector of Dalí, Magritte, and Picasso, sponsor and participant in Mexico's midcentury surrealism. I knew a few survivors of the era, among them an elderly British expatriate writer who'd briefly been James's secretary until he insisted she work in the nude. Then the year before, by sheer coincidence, I'd attended a conference at West Dean, James's former estate in Sussex, now an art college. One damp afternoon, out walking the wide green downs, I'd come upon his spare headstone in a shaded bower. It said, simply, touchingly: EDWARD JAMES. POET. I'd decided it was time to visit Las Pozas.

Eventually the man in the sombrero returned with my change and pointed me back down the road. Carrying an old Super 8 camera I'd brought, I walked in spreading dusk toward a pair of ovoid steel doors. As I passed through them, the common world fell away. An entry path of laid stone ascended between tall rows of mosaic-encrusted serpents, ending at an overhanging cement platform where Edward James's personal palanquin, once borne by workers transporting the old man about Las Pozas, was stored: a yellow chair with a gold silhouette in the shape of a head where his would have rested. A sharp turn upward took me past a pair of waist-high human hands of stone, palms open, planted like flowers beside the path. I heard the chatter of wild parrots, the drip of moisture on fronds, falling water somewhere. There didn't seem to be anyone else in Las Pozas but me.

The climb grew steeper, the shade deeper. I came to a little lotus-shaped platform on which Isadora Duncan might have danced, or Lewis Carroll's caterpillar sat smoking his hookah. I glimpsed, through dense green foliage, twisting, polyplike shapes, fluted columns that looked like giant giraffe legs or organ pipes—whether they were nature's or James's was hard to tell in the advancing darkness. I had no idea when Las Pozas closed, if it closed. But I knew I should turn back soon.

An ascending spiral staircase ended abruptly, leaving me gaping dizzily into space, clutching a fistful of rusted rebars extruding from the unfinished structure like weird tentacles. There was still a little light over the valley below, and I could just see beyond to the town of Xilitla, where already lights were coming on. A giant black butterfly landed on the back of my hand gripping the rebars, fluttered, then glided off toward the valley.

I passed a slatted shed crammed with deserted animal and bird cages, remnants of James's futile dream of a great Noah-like menagerie at Las Pozas. The last thing I remember being able to make out before gloom erased the landscape was a cluster of wooden molds James had used to shape his fantasies, sculptures in their own right.

The drizzle was thickening into rain. I turned back, no longer sure which path I'd taken to get here. I'd dropped down Alice's rabbit hole. I didn't feel afraid—not yet, at least—only lost. A promising fork that led down only turned back up, deeper into jungle. I crossed a bridge over rushing water. Then a slippery descent on stones brought me to a breathless view, through trees, of a waterfall. Silvery light from an unseen source lit the pool at its base. I raised the camera to shoot it.

Then I was on my back, staring up into trees, my head pounding, the base of my spine throbbing. I lay there feeling faint, trying to grasp how I'd fallen, wondering what was damaged. The camera was still in my hand, running, making its little whir. With difficulty I raised my head and looked down the length of my body. My elbows and forearms were badly skinned and starting to bleed. I must have broken my fall with them or my head would have smashed on the stones.

In Mexico your raptures are your own, not prepackaged or branded. The same when things go badly: you're left to your own devices. Nobody to sue, point the accusing finger at; nobody to hold accountable but yourself. I'm comfortable with that view, with its implication that you are, in the deepest sense, responsible for what befalls you. Besides, to pin blame on human or official malfeasance for the pothole you just stepped into in a country like Mexico, where civic matters are a morass and justice unreliable, is an empty exercise. It is easier, perhaps richer, to regard events as guided by something larger, more random; to allow that fate, or chance, routinely intervenes in human affairs; and to recognize that they respond only slightly and occasionally to the imposition of our will. *Ojalá*, people say, meaning the same as the Arabic word from which it is derived, *inshallah*, "God willing." Here in the darkening jungle I couldn't hold the little man in the sombrero, or the ghost of Edward James, or the town of Xilitla responsible for my having slipped on mossy stones. It was I who had chosen to enter the rainy jungle too late in the day. No signs, no map, no brochure, no disclaimers. I could die here, and that would be that. The teeming jungle would make quick work of my remains.

Dazed and nauseous, I hauled myself up. Nothing seemed broken, though my coccyx ached and both legs were sore and wobbly. My forearms, bleeding heavily now, stung. Stepping forward, I almost slipped again. I realized the tread on my old sneakers had worn completely down, offering no traction on the wet stones, causing my fall. I took them off, then my socks, and proceeded unsteadily down the path barefoot, which wasn't much better. I had no idea what slime my feet were finding in the rainy dark.

A random turn dropped me suddenly out onto the access road, further from the entry gate, now closed, of Las Pozas. I could just make out the shape of my car up ahead. Drenched and dizzy, my spine pulsing and sore, I opened the car trunk and fished from my luggage some dry clothes and an old T-shirt to daub my bleeding arms. After I'd changed, I sat in the car for a while, trembling, listening to the rising din of night insects outside. Then I started up the engine, wheeled, and drove back down the muddy road, the headlights flipping up with each bump, sweeping the forest cover above. At the main road I crossed back over the bridge toward Xilitla, where I planned to spend the night.

The road winding up into Xilitla—which is pronounced *shee-LEET-la*—revealed a scrambled, unpretty town clustered on a hill around a long central plaza. The square, lit by arc lights, was filled with brightly colored rides and a little Ferris wheel, all deserted in the rain. Before I'd left San Miguel, I'd called ahead to El Castillo, the house Edward James had built in Xilitla for himself and his lover, Plutarco Gastélum, now operating as a bed and breakfast, and booked a room for two nights. It was easy enough to spot the place, with its soaring turrets and whimsical buttresses, a block off the town square, on a street plummeting toward the valley floor.

I rang the bell at a garden gate and waited. A woman appeared at the door. Crossing the garden separating us, she said, smiling, *"Bienvenido,"* with an American accent. As I followed her across raised stones in the shape of feet—a surrealist trope—a strange sensation filled me. I thought I knew her.

Inside El Castillo, I put my bags down at the foot of stairs flanked by a pair of tall, neo-Egyptian fantasy figures, painted by the British artist Leonora Carrington. Onetime lover of Max Ernst, she had settled in Mexico during the war—and found a friend and patron in Edward James.

The woman was blond, somewhere in her late thirties. She'd told me her name when she opened the door but it hadn't registered. Seeing my condition, she asked if I was okay. I told her briefly of my fall in the jungle, trying to brush aside the feeling of recognition as just a figment of the night, the jungle, the rain, and the surrealist surroundings. A portly, bearded man appeared in the hallway, also American, whom the woman introduced as her husband. He was holding the hand of a little girl of about seven, who announced that she was their daughter,

Elena. She was dark and pretty and looked *indígena*—adopted, I assumed.

I followed my hostess up the stairs to my room, still wondering why she would look familiar. But then people often do; there are, after all, limits to the gallery of human types. If she recognized me, she showed no sign of it. In this odd place, and in my state, nothing made much sense anyway. My head pounded, my arms hurt, and I was much in need of rest, a shower, and a drink.

She opened the door to a corner room with narrow, arched gothic windows facing back across the valley toward Las Pozas, invisible now in the darkness. She asked if I wanted dinner in the hotel. It was raining heavily, and I hadn't seen many places open around Xilitla's empty plaza.

"Yes, thanks," I said.

"Dinner in an hour," she said cheerily. "Drinks downstairs in the salon whenever you're ready."

When she'd left, I took off my shirt, damp with blood from my torn forearms. Showering, I tried again to locate the woman somewhere in my past—but my attention kept diffusing into visions of Edward James's crumbling jungle constructions, my sudden fall, and a damage survey of the cuts and bruises adorning my body.

In the long, dim living room downstairs, a huge, wood-encased console television, very much of the 1950s, stood among furniture to match. I poured myself a tequila at a portable bar and began perusing James's shelves of books. Some were interesting, consonant with what I'd read about him: mysticism, poetry, Kraft-Ebbing, histories of Mexico and of European modernism. Others were surprisingly ordinary, and of his time: *Jonathan Livingston Seagull*, *The Kinsey Report*, Jacqueline Susann's *Valley of the Dolls*. Part of one long shelf was occupied by well-fingered Ludlum and Forsythe thrillers left behind by more recent visitors.

I seemed to be the only guest at El Castillo. The pounding rain and flickering lights made for an ambiance as much Poe as surrealist. On a coffee table I found a copy of a video on James and Las Pozas, made by my hosts apparently, but I was too restless and tired to look at it. I already knew the outlines of James's story.

Born in 1907 to a family of great wealth, rumored to be the illegitimate son of King Edward VII, he'd been part of an Oxford circle of outrageous young aesthetes. When he came into his fortune, he collected and befriended the great avant-garde artists of the day and sometimes appeared in their work. Among his acquaintances and collaborators were Man Ray, Bertolt Brecht, Kurt Weill, Isamu Noguchi, George Balanchine, and Sigmund Freud. He transformed his Sussex estate into a surrealist oddity and showplace. A brief, unconsummated marriage to a well-known dancer, Tilly Losch, ended scandalously, making worldwide headlines; then when a book of his poems was mercilessly panned by reviewers, James fled England for Los Angeles, where in the 1940s and 1950s his friends included Christopher Isherwood, Aldous Huxley, and Igor Stravinsky.

Hearing that Simon Rodia's naïve sculptural masterpiece, *Watts Towers*, was in danger of being razed, James stepped in to help save it.

Meanwhile his burgeoning extravaganza at Las Pozas preoccupied him ever more. With his companion Plutarco and forty workmen, he spent an estimated $10 million from 1962 until his death in 1984 elaborating his jungle fantasia. The photo on the cover of the video—a white-bearded elder in a serape, grinning beside the waterfall I'd been trying to shoot when I'd fallen a few hours earlier—suggested he'd achieved some measure of satisfaction in the end. I did want to see more of his bizarre, eighty-acre Babylonian garden, if I could still move when I awoke in the morning.

Beyond the living room a glassed-in vestibule offered a view of a lit swimming pool on a terrace below, its waters roiled by rain and wind. The aroma of food cooking drew me along a corridor that led back around to the entry hall, where I came to a door opening onto a small kitchen.

The American woman was standing at a sink, rinsing vegetables, her back to me. Seeing me in reflection in the kitchen window, she said, "It's the cook's night off. I'm making your dinner. Come on in, if you like."

I sat down at the kitchen table behind her.

"A French couple booked a room but they haven't shown up," she said. "You're the only guest so far." She turned around, her hands full of peeled carrots, and smiled.

Maybe it was the smile—or the warm, weary blue eyes—

that jarred the recollection. With it came a name—not hers, but the one she'd been with: Eliot.

It was L.A., and I'd arrived there at thirty, broke and with no prospects. After months of scuffling, a friend arranged an interview at a big record company. To my surprise, they hired me to create campaigns for new albums. I stayed a year, and the job saved me from destitution. Eliot was there, working one floor up—a gifted young kid plucked out of Cooper Union to design album covers, posters, T-shirts. Precocious, ultracool, the darling of the art department, he was assigned to the label's best bands.

Yes, it had to be her. And the memory unlocked her name: Jeanine. Eliot and Jeanine.

She'd come out from New York to be with him, as I recalled. Slim and pretty, barely out of her teens, Jeanine was Eliot's golden chick—and in his thrall. Everybody was—at the record company, the clubs, on the streets. Eliot, with his sleek, glam arrogance, his attitude.

For a year we moved in parallel—a milieu of clubs and concerts, superstar openings, recording studios and parties and limos, jetting cross-country just to hear a band. Expense accounts, guest passes, all the fast-lane accoutrements. I was off Eliot's radar; he looked right through me. After all, thirty was old in that culture. I didn't count in their world. Why would she remember me?

She was at the stove, her back to me, stirring a kettle of *sopa de tortilla*. Her fair hair was tangled, unruly. She wore old jeans and a faded, frayed shirt, untucked perhaps to cover a little spreading at the hips. A tired mother and wife here in the far Sierra Madre, with a stolid-appearing husband and an adopted baby daughter, caretaking the house of a dead surrealist.

Six degrees, all that. It wasn't the first time while traveling in Mexico or parts more distant that I'd run into somebody from earlier days. You flee to the ends of the earth, only to bump into a guy from high school. Sometimes the planet isn't so lonely after all.

Echoes of lives outlived, times long left behind. It hadn't been an easy time. A miasma of rock bands, speed, pressure, and sickly excess. I'd exited that scene after a year and hadn't looked back. And what of Eliot? I vaguely recalled hearing he'd gone off to India. Or maybe it was Bali.

Should I bring it up? Maybe it wasn't Jeanine and I was just projecting some dimly recalled scenario that had stayed with me for reasons of my own. If I asked and I was wrong, it would produce awkwardness, cast me in a strange light, leave us alone together in the rainy jungle night in this weird house with a case of mistaken identity. Why stir ghosts when there were plenty on hand already at El Castillo? It had been a crazy time. Their relationship had probably ended badly.

Besides, it isn't as if we'd been friends, only running in the same circles. I looked different now too, time's acid etching age onto the plate of the body. Tired and aching, at the bottom of my tequila, I should probably keep my imaginings to myself. Better to let the past lie.

"Did you ever know somebody named Eliot?"

She was chopping vegetables. Her hands fell still on the cutting board. She looked up at the window above the counter. It was pitch black outside, and I was sitting at an angle to her, so I could see her face clearly in reflection. It was a look I wouldn't forget: as if a sudden incision had been made into annealed flesh.

Maybe it was the solitude, the enforced intimacy. Or some recklessness unleashed by the fall in the jungle, or hunger, or the tequila that had led me to ask. Now we were both trapped with this apparition from the past: lean, caustic, feral Eliot, who didn't belong here in the Sierra Gorda. I felt like an idiot, a sadist. She had the right to remember, and also to choose to forget.

Eliot had been the young, wild love, the extravagant mistake, the crash and burn that leaves you on your knees, desolate and scoured, screaming for succor. It was all there in her face in reflection, running her hand through uncombed hair, staring into the well of time.

She turned to regard the emissary of this terrible question. "Do I know you?"

I filled in the context, quickly and sparingly, trying to bleed it of its disturbing charge: L.A., the record company, those days. "Lifetimes ago," I said. I wanted to apologize for bringing it up, but that would only acknowledge that I recognized what it had stirred up.

She turned back to her cutting board. "Yes," she said tightly. "A long time ago." Cautioning me to go slowly. Or not go at all.

Of course I wanted the rest of the story. Draw me a line from there to here in the jungle. Tell me what happened to Eliot, whom I found hard to wish a good fate. Not that I was going to ask. What moves any of us from point to point? Are our first acts readable in our second ones? In our third? Had she told her husband about Eliot?

Just then he, whose name I did remember—Gardner—walked in.

I could see Jeanine was flustered, uncertain. She was probably worried that I might say something if she didn't—or that if she didn't say anything, it would produce a secret bond between us. She turned to him, hesitated—and in that hesitation I read an emotional encyclopedia—then said, "He knew Eliot."

A scowl flooded Gardner's large, bearded face. "Eliot," he said in a basso profundo of disgust. "A drug-addled, evil bastard."

Clearly Gardner had long ago pronounced his verdict on Eliot, and this was the narrative that prevailed. It said: Do Not Go There.

Too late, I thought, suspecting I'd opened something up that wouldn't close so easily. Now Gardner probably hated me too for bringing this into the space. Yet he had a dilemma, for he knew I was doing a piece for a magazine he'd have liked El Castillo to be in. I'd mentioned it when I'd called to book the room, though I needn't have, as the magazine, to remain free of bias, paid for all lodging and meals. I suppose I'd done it to assure I'd get a good room, the right reception. Obviously if their little surrealist inn was going to survive, they needed to entice more visitors to these faraway mountains. Now Gardner was saddled with a boarder he was supposed to butter up but probably felt like throttling.

I ate alone in the living room, Jeanine bringing me, in turn, *sopa de tortilla, chiles rellenos,* banana cake, a demitasse of local coffee. The only words spoken were her inquiry about the food, and my sincere reply: "Delicious."

After dinner the rain let up. As I was about to go upstairs and disappear into my room, Gardner asked me if I wanted a tour of the place. He walked me to the room next to mine that had been Edward James's; then we climbed to the roof, with its wild, half-finished sculptural extrusions. The rain had let up a little, and there were racing clouds, a three-quarter moon, and a soft breeze running up from the valley.

Gardner, a photographer, had come down here while James was still alive to shoot him. Later he'd made an arrangement with Plutarco's son, who had inherited El Castillo, to lease it and run it as a bed and breakfast. He'd made a video on James that had won a couple of awards and been shown on PBS. Now he was trying to set up a foundation to rehabilitate Las Pozas— shore up the cement structures fast being eaten by the merciless jungle, repaint them in James's original colors, haul out the old wooden forms and recast broken structures. A quixotic scheme, it seemed to me (though I was later to be proven wrong). At some point in the course of their Mexican odyssey, he and Jeanine had adopted the little girl. But how, where, or why Jeanine had come to be with him, and ended up here, remained hidden. Xilitla, and Gardner, were a long way from downtown New York, L.A., the Troubador, the Whisky a GoGo.

Back at the *caracol*, the winding staircase leading down from the roof, Gardner paused. He shot me a heavy, freighted look. "It hasn't been easy," he said. "But we're getting there."

I had no idea what he was alluding to: whether he meant his new foundation, or the little girl, or El Castillo, or his relationship with Jeanine—or existence itself, the whole package. Gardner seemed to be a good man, and I felt cruel for having cast Eliot's shadow into this setting, injecting venom from a distant past.

That night the rain resumed, beating down on the roof. Then it stopped again, and it was quiet in the streets of Xilitla. For a long time there was no sound in El Castillo. Then I heard the bell ring downstairs. It was the French couple, arriving late. I heard Jeanine greet them, then lead them upstairs to a room several doors from mine.

Clever, vain Eliot. Was he even alive now? Did I care? And what of my life back then? Tangled in my own strange drama with Cheryl, who after we split up would check into a sanatorium. From what secure heights did I judge others' affairs and arrangements? For that matter, was my present existence so stable, so clear?

I imagined Jeanine in bed downstairs, thinking to herself: *At least now I have a devoted husband, a beautiful daughter. Eliot was a train wreck. Thank god I got out of that life.* Then turning to sleeping, snoring Gardner and thinking, *And yet . . .*

I'd planned to stay two nights. This might be awkward now. Maybe I should leave in the morning, I thought, and visit the other two Junípero Serra missions before heading on toward Mexico City.

I awoke just before midnight to what seemed like the sounds of raised voices, of arguing. But it could have been the French couple, or the wind that had come up.

4.

Dreamers and Mad Monks

Edward James was hardly the first to discover that you can do things in Mexico you can't do elsewhere. Artists and architects, fascists and fanatics, ascetics and addicts have long known this. Here you can disappear, adopt a new identity, become who you aren't—or who you really are. "We invent a mask," Octavio Paz wrote, "only to discover that the mask is our true identity."

Mexico's physical extravagance—deserts, jungles, mountains, and coasts—seems to invite extremes: cults and *chupacabras*, *calaveras* and consuls run amok; *bandidos*, tyrants, fugitives, and remittance men; *brujería*, *santería*, holy waters, and miracle cancer cures; *angelitos* and *niños muertes*. Certainly Mexico's history could be read as a litany of ruinous excess—from Mayan and Aztec blood rites to the rapacious Conquest to the penitents of Atotonilco; from Porfirio Díaz's imperial fin de siècle luxuriance to the murderous revolution that followed in reaction; from Emiliano Zapata to Frida and Diego to the

Tijuana drug cartels. Here André Breton found himself completely outflanked by Mexico's innate surrealism and admitted it; here William Burroughs put a bullet in his wife's head and walked away free.

In Mexico all manner of exiles, émigrés, and expatriates have found shelter—from Trotsky to Fidel, from Luis Buñuel to García Marquez, from the Shah of Iran to Howard Hughes. Ex-revolutionaries, deposed dictators, old Nazis and anarchists grow old together on plaza benches in baggy pants, feeding the pigeons. In Mexico, Robert Rodriguez concocts cinema fairy tales of blood orgies and terminal violence—*El Mariachi, Once Upon a Time in Mexico*—in which the country is both paradise and badlands. Here strangeness may be noted but not censured. There's nothing a little *mordida*, *la pica*, the bite, can't arrange. Here you don't need no stinking badges.

So Mexico stands in the foreign imagination: as a permanently exotic, lawless, and untamed antidote to the gray sterility of its northern neighbor. If in fact most Mexicans' lives are little different from those of their northern neighbors—jobs, family worries, discount shopping malls—and if gradually the country comes under the rule of civil law, Mexico still plays to North America as its collective unconscious, its Dionysian Other: land of *salsa* and *sabor*, fiestas and revelry, ghosts and gore. A country riddled with bullet holes and beauty.

On the day that was to end with my fall in the jungle, and my strange encounter with Jeanine at El Castillo, I'd left San Miguel early, hoping to get to Jalpan, the capital of the Sierra

Gorda, by lunchtime. Driving south toward Mexico City, I'd turned east at Bernál, a little tourist town best known for the great rock that towers over it, and followed a two-lane road across a patch of barren plateaus. A hairpin ascent led through dry, silvery, cactus-dotted scarp. Gradually the mountains softened into alpine forests near the summit before snaking down into lush forests of banana, tamarind, bougainvillea, and poinsettia.

A sequestered, little-touristed region of mountains and subtropical valleys, meandering rivers and hamlets, the Sierra Gorda is nestled within the greater eastern Sierra Madre range that divides central Mexico from the Caribbean coast. When in 1750 the Franciscan monk Junípero Serra came to this region to save souls, he made the trip from Mexico City in sixteen days on foot—a five-hour trip by car nowadays. He spent eight years here, building five missions within a day's walk of each other and preaching in the local Pame tongue—an interlude, it would turn out, before moving on to the grand project that would crown his tireless, troubling passage through the New World: the construction of the great chain of missions along the California coast, from San Diego to San Francisco, that would define the emergent state.

Anyone familiar with coastal California knows the kindly, benevolent image of "Father Serra." Growing up among those spacious, unadorned, tile-roofed white missions, I was imprinted early with the prevailing image of the man: a portly, tonsured monk in brown cowl, writing in a journal with a quill

pen, or astride a burro en route to his next mission—exemplar
of the benign, scholarly, industrious, celibate monk. This semi-
specious portrait was, of course, ripe for revision: the monastic
orders that swept through the New World were preceded, and
sustained, by conquering armies that destroyed; and the horri-
ble, ironic consequence of the evangelizing project was the ex-
termination, by violence or disease, of the very souls they'd
come to save. Serra's pending election to sainthood, deeply opposed by American Indian groups, among others, was steeped
in controversy.

Before sailing to Mexico the summer of 1749, Serra had
been a professor of theology on his native island of Mallorca, a
disciple of the medieval Catalan alchemist and mystic Ramon
Llull. Landing in Veracruz, he walked, with his companion and
future biographer Friar Palou, all the way to Mexico City. At
the capital's Franciscan headquarters, San Carlos, plans were already under way to evangelize the Pame natives of the Sierra
Gorda. Serra volunteered for the job and the following spring
set out for the region's main town, Jalpan. He was thirty-seven
years old.

Few know about, much less have seen, the five missions the
indefatigable friar built in the Sierra Gorda. I'd heard they were
different from the California ones but wasn't prepared for what
I'd find. Rounding a turn, I saw a little town below on a bluff in
a smoky valley surrounded by low green mountains, gathered
around the largest structure in sight: Santiago de Jalpan, Serra's
first mission.

It was early on a Saturday afternoon when I climbed out of the VW into soft, sweet air. Chattering grackles crowded the laurel trees around Jalpan's broad plaza. I passed through the mission gates into the wide *atrio*, the forecourt, and stood among children and dogs, gazing up at the facade, astonished.

Restorers had recently repainted the weather-beaten surfaces in ocher, burnt sienna, and terra cotta, following Serra's original color plan, revealing narrative detail lost for centuries— restoring the florid, even lurid, palette of a pictorial extravaganza. A swarming, phantasmagorical sea of imagery jumped out at me—six soaring tiers of opulent Christian narrative interleaved with indigenous myths and fancies. Animals, cherubs, and angels lurked in niches. Leaves and fruits entwined gargoyle faces. The arms of Saint Francis and a friar were nailed together on a cross. A double-headed eagle devoured a serpent (an image found in both Aztec symbology and the Austrian Hapsburg crest). A storybook in stone: high Baroque hallucinations. Nothing could have been further from Serra's severe, undecorated California missions.

People were slowly emerging from the church after mass. I slipped among them through the carved entry door into the chapel, thinking how it would have pleased Serra to see such a crowd; for only a dozen years after his departure, the missions had fallen into disuse and disrepair ("invaded by silence," as one Mexican author put it). Inside, fanciful biblical scenes and delicate floral decorations in reds and greens, hand-painted by Pame artisans, adorned the sacristy walls, mixing Christian and pre-Hispanic themes. This, the largest of the missions Serra built in the Sierra Gorda, had taken him and his artisans seven years to complete.

I emerged into sharp sunlight, scattering pigeons. Across the street a thick-walled adobe fort that had once housed the friars was a mission museum now, full of artifacts and displays of the monks' formidable array of skills: carpentry, painting, gardening, agronomy, surveying. Serra's tiny room, with a simple wooden bed overhung by a cross, was nearly identical to the one at Carmel Mission, his California headquarters, where he would end his days.

Back in the VW, I followed a languid river valley through countryside rich with plantain, jacaranda, ocotillo cacti. Citrus fragrance swept the car. After half an hour I came to the tiny farming hamlet of Concá, surrounded by green valleys and mountains, gathered around little Misión San Miguel Arcángel. Its freshly restored facade was no less fantastical than Jalpan's: Saint Michael slaying a monster, religious and political luminaries of the day occupying niches, winged angels guarding the central scalloped window. Inside, the simple chapel breathed warmth and artistry—simulated lace hand-stenciled in blue on the walls, brightly colored bas-relief fruits decorating the ceiling.

Back outside in the mission forecourt, I stood at a low adobe wall, gazing at a river winding through cultivated fields below, blue mountains beyond, captivated by the region's beauty as much as by Serra's missions. I hadn't known, or even imagined, such an area existed in Mexico. Here was its Napa Valley, its Provence, its Tuscany, undiscovered and undeveloped. I was beginning to sense the spell the Sierra Gorda had cast upon these two earlier voyagers whose traces in stone and cement I'd come to find.

The road from Concá led back to Jalpan, then east to the Mission Virgin Mary at Landa. Banked up against soft green mountains on one side, open to rolling blue-green countryside on the other, Landa was even lovelier than the first two missions, its facade more fanciful: mermaids, a man being hanged, a jester with an upside-down head, bas-reliefs of saints Peter and Paul and Francis, angels with European musical instruments wearing pre-Columbian feather headdresses; eagles, tigers, jaguars, rabbits, snails—a fabulous Boschian bestiary. I suspected the medieval alchemical doctrines of Ramon Llull were tucked in there too if only I could read them. But what messages did the Pame Indians whom Serra had come so far to convert possibly draw from this mad visual cornucopia?

Junípero Serra, secret artist and voluptuary. So much for the mild monk of Carmel. Like Edward James two centuries later, he'd gone wild in the Sierra Gorda. Was it something in the air, some elixir circulating among these loping valleys and hills that looked like biblical illustrations of the promised land? Was it the robust talents of Pame artisans, unleashed by the encounter with the new, imposed doctrine, that had produced this artistic efflorescence, teeming with imagination and emotion? Or a driven, energetic new team of friars? How to explain

Serra's later lean West Coast minimalism? Did he tire, mellow out? Were the California Indians less inclined to make art? Was he under stricter orders, on a tighter budget?

There were two more missions to visit, but each was a distance from the main road. It was getting late, and I was already brimming with impressions. Coming to the end of the radiant valley, I descended two thousand feet into muggy rainforest, heading for my ill-fated twilight tumble at Edward James's jungle garden, Las Pozas.

The next morning I awoke late at El Castillo to find the room bathed in pale light. Willing myself out of bed through a blizzard of aches, I stepped out onto the narrow balcony. Mist was burning off over Las Pozas, sun illuminating the peak above.

Hoping to avoid Jeanine and Gardner after the awkwardness of the night before, I slipped downstairs and out the door unnoticed. I took coffee and churros on Xilitla's sunlit plaza, then climbed back in the mud-spattered VW. Twenty minutes later I was again at the gates of Las Pozas, handing the little man in the sombrero eight pesos.

Sunlight dappled the jungle floor through a netting of philodendrons, palms, and wild orchids. Las Pozas seemed cheerful and festive today, its somber twilit aspect erased. Wearing fresh shoes, and armed with a brochure and map Gardner had left under my door, I entered again through the strange ovoid doors, ascending what I now read James had named the

Serpent's Walk. A tangle of paths drew me back into Las Pozas's dank mysteries. Exoskeletons of crumbling structures winked through the foliage. Soon I was lost again in a collage of artistic quotes, consulting the map to no avail. Was I near the Homage to Max Ernst, the Homage to Henry Moore? The Parrot House? The House with a Roof Curved like a Whale? Where was the Tank Like an Eye, the Bamboo Palace? Did I care? Logic's compass had broken. Enmeshed in James's forest hermitage, a dream garden of light and birdsong, my affinity for the man soared. Did it matter that he'd left Las Pozas unfinished, or that the jungle was reclaiming it? I could almost hear the bearded old man in the serape chuckling in my ear: *It's all folly anyway, isn't it, the works of man? Let's take a little pleasure along the way!*

At one point I crossed the bridge of the night before, arriving at the spot where I'd tried to video the waterfall and fallen. I saw, across a leafy ravine, the cascade plummeting into the glistening pool where in 1945 James had seen his traveling companion Plutarco naked in a cloud of butterflies and decided to buy the old coffee finca. Mexican kids were swimming in the pool, shouting and laughing. I thought I heard the voices of the French couple who had arrived late to El Castillo the night before, though I couldn't see them. Descending by a series of slippery paths, past whimsical sculptural forms James had built into stone alcoves, I reached the pool at the base of the waterfall, peeled off my outer clothes, and waded in.

Around midday, back at the palapa stand, I ate a tamale and drank a *refresco*. Then, still in the grips of Las Pozas, I wandered back into the jungle by way of another path, emerging only when the first shadows of dusk gathered in the forest cover above me.

That evening I lingered around the square in Xilitla, thinking it might be best to return to El Castillo later, allowing any lingering discomfort from the revelations of the evening before to dispel. I wouldn't have minded talking more to Jeanine, if only to learn how she'd come so far from Hollywood and Eliot, but figured this wasn't going to happen and probably shouldn't; instead I feared Gardner would draw me aside for a heart-to-heart, implicating me further in whatever my appearance the night before might have stirred up between them.

It was a Sunday evening in the town, under dry skies, and families were enjoying the rides rained out the night before. Balloon merchants and *paleteros* selling ice cream roamed the plaza among boys and girls doing the ancient courting perambulation, the *paseo*. If Xilitla didn't look much prettier, it was warmer and livelier—though as in so many Mexican towns these days, there were too many *mujeres* alone, their men driven north across the border to work.

At nightfall I found a restaurant a block off the plaza and took a table at the back by a wide window facing the valley. Sipping tall Pacificos and nibbling *enchiladas suizas*, I let time pass, delaying my arrival back at the hotel. The restaurant began to fill with cowboys, families, and old-timers. Then the lights dimmed and a live Huastecan trio began to play, their fast little *requinto* guitars and agile, high-pitched, emotive singing owing as much to the Caribbean as to central Mexico. I ordered another cerveza and listened, feeling far from San Miguel de Allende now, and the life I knew there—deep in another Mexico.

A few summers back a band from this Huasteca region, Los Leones de Xichú, had visited San Miguel and played to a packed audience on folding chairs at the Syndicato, the local union building. Lead singer Guillermo Velásquez, a kind of Mexican Woody Guthrie who composes lyrics on the spot full of biting wit and social observation, had sung of entering a couple of pricey art galleries in San Miguel but feeling he, a simple Mexican, didn't belong there. When he sang *"En San Miguel Allende / A donde se compra, a donde se vende,"* the audience erupted in laughter and recognition. "In San Miguel / Where they buy and they sell." Velásquez's couplet had struck a nerve.

In the Xilitla restaurant, a couple got up and danced. The girl, with her cropped hair, flowered dress, and gamine frame, looked eerily like Cheryl, whom I'd been with when I'd first met Jeanine and Eliot. How strange, all this: Serra and James, Eliot and Jeanine. What *wasn't* surreal? Clearly I had my own ghosts to put down. The year before in Los Angeles I'd attended a memorial service for gifted, fragile Cheryl, who hadn't made it out of her forties.

I arrived back at the gate to El Castillo a little after nine and rang the bell. Jeanine's daughter Elena let me in.

In the living room a family of Texans was sprawled over the 1950s couch, watching the Edward James video on the giant TV console. The French couple was looking at books. I was about to slip upstairs when Jeanine appeared from the kitchen, carrying serving platters in both hands.

She'd washed her hair, put on makeup and lipstick, and donned earrings and a long black dress. Her face was flushed, her eyes a little swollen—from weeping, perhaps? I sensed, or thought I did, that all this was mixed up with the Eliot business of the night before, and that she'd done this for herself—an act of shoring up, but maybe also for me, possibly a little embarrassed at having been come upon by someone from those glamour days in her housewifely guise. She looked, and didn't look, like the girl I remembered: in fact, she looked better.

She paused, platters in hand, not quite looking at me, and said, "I went to India with Eliot. Things got pretty crazy. I left him in Benares." She turned as if to move on toward the living room, then stopped again. "I just wanted you to know that—"

Her daughter came running up and grabbed her dress.

Jeanine shrugged, smiled, looked fondly down at Elena. "Well. It doesn't matter anymore. Does it?"

"No, not at all," I said. "I'm truly sorry I brought it up."

"You're leaving in the morning?"

"Yes, early."

"Well . . ." She held up the platters as if to indicate she couldn't shake hands. "Good luck."

"Thanks. You too."

My eyes followed hers up to the strange, surreal Leonora Carrington wall paintings beside the stairs.

"Last I heard he was back in New York," she said.

"Eliot?"

"Yeah."

Then she tossed her head slightly, as if to say *c'est la vie* and fuck him, and swept on toward her guests.

Upstairs I packed everything before turning in, hoping to get an early start, visit the last two of Serra's missions, then make it out of the Sierra Gorda by dark.

By midmorning I was out of the rainforest and back up on the valley floor, traveling a secluded dirt road past sunlit cornfields and blue hills. At Mission St. Francis of Assisi at Tilaco, set in a tiny agrarian settlement, a statue of the gentle saint gazed down from the massive facade, surrounded by carved flowers, angels, and animals. A lone, white-bearded Catalan monk, Fray Milagros (Brother Miracles), looked after Tilaco's few parishioners in this setting of unearthly beauty. Seeing the aged friar at the desk of his office in the cloister counseling a youth, I was disinclined to interrupt him or the silence and peace enveloping Tilaco. I got back in the car and headed for the fifth and last mission.

The straight paved streets around Mission Tancoyol seemed almost urban after rural Tilaco. Dedicated to Our Lady of Light, it featured on its facade an astonishing rendering after Giotto: a Jesus on a cross beaming bloody stigmata lines to the body of a floating Saint Francis. Begun in 1761, Tancoyol wasn't finished until late in the decade, by which time Serra had left the Sierra Gorda.

Crossing Tancoyol's grassy forecourt on the way out, I felt the grip of my two days in the region loosening. Perhaps Serra had felt this sensation as he prepared to return to Mexico City for reassignment, little knowing the arduous journey, and greater task, that lay ahead. With the expulsion of the Jesuits from New Spain, orders had come to secularize all their missions; the Franciscans were put in charge of former Jesuit outposts in Sonora and the Californias—hence Serra's recall from the Sierra Gorda and his fateful journey north to San Diego in 1769.

Driving back across the valley floor toward Jalpan, I wondered what to make of a man like Junípero Serra. Or for that matter Edward James, equally driven by the compulsions of his time. James, with his surrealist gardens, pet snakes, and nude secretaries; Serra, with his mystical theology, his mission-building mania, and his languages. One a passionate lover of art, the other a fervent harvester of souls. Serra, for whom religion expressed itself in near-art; James, to whom art was as a religion.

Or seen in another light: two decadent egotists, one a zealous exterminator of indigenous populations, spreading medieval ecclesiasticism's last foul breath into the new hemisphere; the other modernism's mad messiah, a frivolous artist *manqué* who squandered millions on his quirky, unfinished hymn to futility.

As I wound down the steep mountain face leading out of the Sierra Gorda, the twentieth-century aesthete's benefaction seemed as pure—or impure—to me as the eighteenth-century

Franciscan friar's. Which was the sybarite, which the monk? In my imagination they'd traded aspects: Junípero Serra the artist, Edward James the renunciant, their peculiar legacies in cement and stone improbably juxtaposed, or intertwined, in those remote Mexican mountains. Their edifices, unlike the film sets of *Once Upon a Time in Mexico*, weren't built to be struck. (Not long after my visit, thanks to Gardner and Jeanine's efforts, a U.S. museum would undertake to sponsor the restoration and preservation of Las Pozas.)

Serra and James, revered and reviled. Saintly visionaries or grotesque megalomaniacs? Holy men or fools? Or some unnerving combination? As I pulled into the lowlands village and spa of Tequisquiápan at dusk, I felt no more certain than when I'd entered the Sierra Gorda. Still everything had changed somehow.

But lying in bed that night in a local inn, it wasn't James, or Serra—but Jeanine, Eliot, and Cheryl—whose apparitions trailed me into sleep.

5.

City of Mud

*"What I thought was the dead had come
back to life. I realized that while I had
believed that I was walking over a cemetery
of a culture, the culture had been abiding
beneath my feet."*

—CARLOS FUENTES

In Mexico City I still sleep with my shoes, pants, and wallet next to the door. At least when I remember to, I do. I'm sure others who lived through the 1985 earthquake go through similar rituals—even if mine, with its suggestion of running out into the street with nothing but shoes and pants and wallet, makes for a strange, cartoonish, completely inadequate response to an event that exceeds human control in any case.

Raised along California's San Andreas Fault, I'd lived through my share of *temblores*, *sismos*, and *terremotos*. Back home

I'd stared up at ceilings sprouting a netting of cracks, tumbled to the floor among books and crockery, listened to car sirens and dogs' howls spread like a tide across a shuddering landscape, watched chimneys separate from houses. I'd felt the earth move under my feet for reasons other than love. But the Mexico City quake, all three-plus minutes of it, stayed with me as no other had. The capital still suffers tremors regularly, but none to equal that one: twenty to thirty thousand dead the final reckoning, though nobody really knows how many fell that September morning. Fifty-six thousand buildings destroyed or damaged, a half million left homeless. Rubble was still being excavated years later, and gaps on the city map mark leveled neighborhoods that will never be rebuilt. To Mexico City, already reeling from crime, poverty, overpopulation, corruption, and toxic contamination, the 1985 earthquake heaped injury upon insult. El Temblor changed the face of the city, and also its heart.

After the curious idyll in the Sierra Gorda and the night in Tequisquiápan, I approached Mexico City from the north on Highway 57, which runs all the way from Texas. Shortly after the last tollbooth, still forty-five minutes shy of the city proper, visibility clouded, traffic thickened, and a metallic taste hit my tongue. Where a few years earlier there had been open country, ranchos, a wide blue horizon, and scudding clouds, now factories and new shantytown *colonias* crowded the roadside. Passing the great stone statue of Jesus rising against a barren hill on my left, I entered fetid, snarled Mexico City, once the site of resplendent Aztec Tenochtitlán, which had struck awe in the Spanish conquistadores who beheld it.

It hadn't always been this bad. Fifty years ago Mexico appeared to be on its way to first-world prosperity. With seeming limitless resources—huge oil reserves newly discovered in the gulf, boundless human capital ready to work, a burgeoning educated class, a populist government with an enlightened international policy, and no foreign enemies, the arts of Rivera and Orozco and Kahlo and the architecture of Luis Barragán, and recent discoveries of a brilliant early Mayan civilization on display in a thrilling new anthropology museum in the city's leafy Chapultepec Park—Mexico seemed to have it all. Movies of the time—still replayed constantly on Mexican television, distressingly poignant in the light of what has since happened—show handsome modern families living Technicolor lives in roomy ranch-style Mexico City houses, the women with Doris Day bobs, the men in tan golf slacks cruising the Paseo de la Reforma in Chevy convertibles and Thunderbirds. Tony neighborhoods—Lomas, Polanco, Pedregal, San Ángel—celebrated the new affluence with grand dwellings and shaded parks. The air was clear, oil was flowing, and the capital was cool and cultured and au courant. Nothing was more stylish than a honeymoon in Acapulco; and when Liz, Richard, Ava Gardner, and John Huston made *The Night of the Iguana*, turning sleepy Puerto Vallarta into an international hot spot, Mexico seemed to own the future.

From there, things slid rapidly downhill. Oil wealth, nominally in the hands of the government, disappeared into private pockets. With little capital invested in the countryside, Mexico's broad agrarian base eroded, driving workers into the cities or north to the United States. The PRI, which had taken power after the revolution, was now as corrupt and sclerotic as the Soviet politburo, operating with utter scorn for its constituency, funding outrageous schemes, or spiriting the national wealth abroad. As rural people flooded in from the countryside, Mexico City's population swelled from four to fifteen million in a few decades. Industrial pollution, car exhaust, and fecal matter turned the air nearly lethal. In 1968, on the eve of the Mexico City Olympics, a brutal massacre of university students in Tlacelolco Plaza exposed Mexico's unaddressed contradictions to the world. The peso collapsed, again and again. Development ground to a halt. Mexico, its coffers stripped bare, was in hock to foreign interests.

The earthquake of 1985 was the coup de grâce, driving a stake into the heart of the old order. The government's response—denial, delay, silence, leaving ordinary people and international volunteers to dig through the rubble—lost it any last shred of respect. The aftershocks, physical and social, have never fully subsided. Mexico City became a featureless ocean of slum neighborhoods, glue sniffers, flame eaters, and wheezing children—*los olvidados*, the lost ones: the urban nightmare incarnate. *Capitalinos*, nearly twenty million of them now, fell prey to epic waves of crime and kidnappings, often at the hands of the police themselves, the rich protecting their distance with bulletproof limousines and fleets of armed security guards.

I streamed onto Avenida Avila Camacho among belching buses, past grimy brick buildings and street vendors, the pressure of airborne particulate matter throbbing behind my eyes, the horizon erased, the air soup. Heading for the hotel where I planned to spend the night before leaving by plane for Oaxaca the next morning, I recalled bringing a well-traveled friend to the city for the first time and her saying as we drove this stretch, "This is the ugliest city I've ever seen." I had no answer but to try to guide her to places that might temper her first impression.

For all its wretched aspects, there were those who reveled in the city. Like the scavengers who work the capital's great garbage dumps, these bottom-feeders found here a bleak poetry: the city as glimmering, irradiated underworld. My film critic friend Eduardo, whom I was to meet for dinner that night, wouldn't dream of living anywhere else. He reveled in the grit and vitality, the cantina life that abounded in the face of ruin, the anarchic punk nihilism that suffused the culture, the edgy satire that prevailed under such conditions. To him, this was the East Village in the 1970s, or Henry Miller's down-and-out Paris of the 1930s, full of cackling laughter and dead-end despair. Such trolls and troglodytes as emerged from the imagination in a city of total hopelessness and defeat stirred him. Like others here, he prided himself on having cut a path through another impossible day without getting mugged, hassled, or shot—or in spite of having suffered them.

The art of base survival quickened these dwellers of the lower depths: to such anatomists of decay, all the room was, as Henry Miller once wrote, at the bottom. I had gay friends who loved the night scene of cabaret and drag, equally the spectacle of art, opera, and dance at the grand old theater and cultural center, Bellas Artes. For Mexico City was, in spite of it all and paradoxically—I tried to explain this to my repelled friend that evening in the time-worn Bar Ópera downtown—steeped in culture.

When I first lived in Mexico, the closest airport was Benito Juárez in Mexico City, a four-or-five-hour bus ride from San Miguel. I was a regular visitor to the capital and often stayed over a night or two in the old downtown district off the Zócalo, the great central square, at a succession of then modestly priced hotels: the Majestic, where Edward James's pet boa constrictor had once escaped from its cage; the Monte Carlo, where D. H. Lawrence had famously put up; the Isabel, near where Mexico's great poet Sor Juana had held forth in her nunnery until Inquisition pressures forced her to cease writing; the Ritz, with its mural above the bar by the virtuoso illustrator and anthropologist Miguel Covarrubius; the Cortéz, a former monastery; the Del Prado on the Alameda, where Diego Rivera's lavish mural of Mexican society took up an entire side of the lobby until the quake destroyed the hotel; or the Regis, where retired theater folk who had been living there perished when the building collapsed into rubble that awful morning.

It was in this once-elegant neighborhood of narrow streets, Baroque palaces, and tiled buildings that Henri Cartier-Bresson and Langston Hughes roomed together one youthful summer in 1934; at the venerable Café Tacuba where the sociologist Oscar Lewis found the subjects for his landmark study *The Children of Sanchez*. The quarter is full of such commemorative traces. I too felt the romance of ruin among the sagging colonial buildings, the dust of decay, the traces of successive cultures that had been conquered or simply foundered here. At Café La Blanca on Avenida Cinco de Mayo, waiters in soiled white jackets hovered against the walls as if time had simply expired; ex-prostitutes with orange hair and plucked eyebrows, poured into dresses that could no longer contain them, sat at the counter sipping *tequilas blancos*; old gentlemen in frayed suits, faces flayed by tobacco, stirred *cafés con leche*, unfiltered Delicados burning down in Corona ashtrays. At the *escritorios* nearby, shabby clerks sat behind old Smith Coronas tapping out deeds, wills, or love letters for the city's illiterate. In the tragic, crumbling *centro*, I found respite from the bustling, ordered vacuity of stateside life—breathing room, however implausibly, in this choking, wheezing city.

Like everyone in *el D.F.*, as Mexicans call their capital— short for Distrito Federal—I was always trying to read through the present to the past, to discern in the broken visage what had once been whole. Out in the once-quiet neighborhood of Coyoacán, by the deep blue *azul añil* wall of Frida Kahlo's house, I was back fifty years with Trotsky, Siqueiros, Diego, and Frida. On a bench in Alameda Park, fending off urchins hawking *chicles*, I was among the horse-drawn carriages, parasols, and flashing swords of the French-Spanish society that had built it. Sometimes I liked to cross the Zócalo between the National Palace and the massive cathedral to the great excavation site of the Templo Mayor, the old Mexica ceremonial center, and gaze at the reconstructed model of the ancient city with its lakes and canals, its earthworks of reed and mud called *chinampas* on which Aztec Tenochtitlán once floated. "Now all that I saw then has vanished," wrote Cortés's chronicler Bernal Díaz in 1559, forty years after the invasion. "Strewn, lifeless, destroyed forever." How much violation can a city take and still exist?

The Metropolitan Cathedral on the Zócalo, the largest in Latin America, which took more than two hundred years to build, is sinking into the mud of Lake Texcoco. Far below ground engineers are drilling holes in its base to let in the mud in hopes that it will compress and stabilize the 127,000-pound structure—a plan originally devised to right the Tower of Pisa. Above ground, among those somber, dank chapels that are still open, green scaffolding and sheaths of draped plastic lend it the appearance of a Christo installation. In the ooze far below, eerily visible to the engineers working down there, is a stone circle surrounded by four smaller ones, enclosed in a square, its blue and red pigment still intact: an Aztec calendar from the Temple of the Sun, on top of which Cortés commanded the church to be built. Mexican troglodytes, lurking down there, ancient gods peering up from the depths to disquiet the contemporary mind, sucking the city back into the muck on which it was vaingloriously erected.

The hotel I frequented most in those days was the Guardiola on Calle Madero, across from Sanborn's House of Tiles, with its ample, spare rooms and huge art deco chandelier in the open central stairwell. It was there that the writer Paul Bowles had once waited vainly for his new bride Jane to arrive, unaware that she'd run off with another woman. And it was at the

Guardiola that I'd awakened the morning of the earthquake, checking out only minutes before it ceased to exist. Though I rarely stayed downtown anymore, I'd since found myself more than once back on Calle Madero, staring at the boarded-up, condemned structure, communing with ghosts.

I turned onto Calle Álvaro Obregón, a boulevard divided by trees and wrought-iron benches, and pulled into the garage of the Hotel Milan, relieved to be off the road. In recent years, when passing through the city, I usually put up at this small, serviceable, nondescript hotel in the district known as Roma, with its quiet rooms, fading posters of modernist art on the walls, and 1950s-era restaurant downstairs. If the neighborhood lacked the high drama and majesty of downtown, it was easier to get to, had a corner café I liked, and was directly across the street from the Casa Lamm, a literary and cultural center filled with books and magazines. And Colonia Roma, at least in theory, rested on more solid ground than the centro.

Fetching a key in the lobby, I grabbed a newspaper from a pile of them, rode the tiny elevator up to my room, and set down my bags. Then as if to announce my descent from the remote Sierra Gorda, the world came flooding back in as a headline: my country had invaded Afghanistan. Mexico, expressing its outrage along with the rest of the world, had filled the Zócalo the day before with tens of thousands of protesters. More demonstrations were planned for the days to come.

I sat on the bed, stunned. The attack, if hardly unexpected, was a *temblor* all the world would feel, its consequences echoing and spreading in unforeseen ways. Americans moving in the world would, whether they wished to or not, be held answerable for this.

Early that evening, still in a daze, I left the hotel and walked across the street to the Casa Lamm, where I was to meet Eduardo. Entering through the tall gates of the onetime private residence, I descended stairs and passed through a narrow doorway into a world of books, music, and magazines for sale or for browsing. In this subterranean warren of rooms, filled with comfortable couches and reading tables, I could briefly indulge the sense that culture can, if not fend off ruin, then at least respond to it creatively. Mexico had always found money for the arts when so much else in the land was scarcity. In this city, founded upon an invasion, where the ancestral Mexica peered up at the present through ruins, a passionate connection to poetry and art survived. Among the hundreds of books arrayed about the shelves and tables, the first one my eye fell upon was a new edition of Bernal Díaz's history of the conquest.

"Welcome to this oasis in a sea of madness."

I turned to find Eduardo grinning at me.

"There's a little restaurant in the Condesa," he said. "Shall we?"

Outside I fell into step with Eduardo as he bounded along the cracked pavement, jacket tails flying. A film reviewer for a leading Mexico City daily, he was a *sesenta y ocho*, one of those who had lived through the student massacre of 1968. In his jeans, sneakers, and rumpled jacket, with his droopy mustache and hand-rolled cigarettes, he presented an image of the eternal, incorruptible graduate student, even as silver hairs had begun to infest his untended mane. Undying Mexico City loyalist and eager informant, Eduardo always managed to make me love the city a little when I was with him.

"Demonstrations," he said, "leave me ravenous."

"The Zócalo?"

"Yeah, another big one." He glanced at me gravely. "It's not like we're totally against you. Over a hundred Mexicans died in the World Trade Center that morning—janitors on the early shift, mostly. But Bush is squeezing us about this 'coalition of the willing' shit, and President Fox is falling for it. The protest is as much against Fox as Bush. We need immigration reform and trade talks with you guys, not war. And what does going into Afghanistan solve?" He spread his arms. "U.S. invasions are a sensitive subject around here."

Repeated U.S. incursions into the "halls of Montezuma," including the occupation of Mexico City from 1846 to 1848— episodes mostly forgotten in the States—lived on in the Mexican public mind: each year the Niños Heroes, schoolboys who leaped to their deaths from the parapets of Chapultepec Castle rather than surrender to North American soldiers, were recalled and celebrated in a national holiday.

Eduardo guided us down a quiet, leafy Condesa street to a sidewalk restaurant table. We ordered a couple of beers and *carne asada*. A trendy young man passed by wearing an earring and a Che Guevera T-shirt, leading Eduardo to mention, rather caustically, that Che's book *The Motorcycle Diaries*, recounting his youthful trip around South America, was about to be made into a movie. The role of Che—or El Che, as he's known in the Spanish-speaking world—was to be played by Gael García Bernal, the young star of *Amores Perros*, the recent international hit about life in the underbelly of Mexico City. When I told Eduardo I hoped to make a trip to Bolivia, Chile, and Peru the following year, he began to tell me, with great relish, of a recent incident at Casa Lamm.

"They threw a little reception for Bolivia's new ambassador to Mexico, a onetime military man now in a wheelchair from a bullet wound. At one point an older Mexican journalist—I know the guy, actually—burst in, threw a glass of wine in the crippled man's face, asked how he could have the gall to represent his country to Mexico, and demanded his recall. It turned out the new ambassador had been with the infamous army and CIA team that hunted down El Che in the Bolivian mountains and executed him point-blank."

The killing, on October 9, 1967, in a tiny schoolhouse in the village of La Higuera, was an event in contemporary Latin American history as defining as the Kennedy assassination in the United States. Photos taken in death after the capture—the Jesus-like crucifixion pose, arms spread, lean and pale, with his light beard and pretty eyes, lit like a Caravaggio—assured Che Guevara's ascension to public immortality.

"The wineglass assailant, an old-time Mexican Communist, considered the man's appointment an intolerable insult to Mexico. The Latin American Left may be on the ropes, but they're going down swinging. So did our government kick Ambassador Prado out? No, they apologized to Bolivia instead!"

We laughed, if a little uneasily, at this quaint, parochial incident. It seemed comic, also emblematic somehow, as the world changed about us quickly now, forging new icons in its fires. I asked Eduardo if he thought Osama Bin Laden was the next Che.

"El Che . . ." Eduardo said ruminatively. "To the gringo he's just a defeated romantic, a mere socialist. To a Mexican— any Latin American—he is all that is beautiful in us, all that is damned."

As we attacked our *carne asada*, I thought how we North Americans tend to dismiss anything smacking of futility or defeat. Latin Americans, half-children of Don Quixote, understand in Che's failure the truth of the proposition that, as little or nothing comes of things anyway, it is the noble gesture, not the result, that redeems a life.

"You have the Terminator," Eduardo said. "We have El Che—the Terminated!" Chuckling, he shoved his plate aside and lit a hand-rolled cigarette. "Like Jesus Christ, also terminated."

Along the street, traffic had died down. An organ grinder serenaded a table in the restaurant next to ours.

"See, El Che is the real thing," Eduardo said, unwilling yet to abandon the subject. "He actually lived and died. The Terminator is unborn, hence undead—in the Hollywood way. Instead, Schwarzenegger lives on to become governor of your state!"

Now Eduardo had us both laughing. We paid our check and rose to leave.

"No, Osama is not the next Che," he said. "Maybe he's bigger."

We walked the quiet, darkened streets back to the Hotel Milan. Headlights refracting through pollution cast orange haloes into the wilting trees along Álvaro Obregón. Traversing a deserted, unlit block, I asked Eduardo if he felt safe walking at night in Mexico City.

"Safer than in a taxi. See this?" He craned his neck to show me a red stripe of skin. "Last summer in the Zona Rosa I got in a cab. Two other guys jumped in, hit me a few times, put a knife to my throat. Local cops. They drove me to a cash machine nearby. Stupid guys, to pick a film critic. My account was overdrawn!"

Eduardo's gallows humor helped me suppress the urge to look back over my shoulder.

"So did you hear? We hired Rudolph Giuliani to come here and clean up Mexico City the way he cleaned up New York. Good luck, Rudy! Our media has been in stitches over that one."

Back alone in my room at the Milan, I discovered I was a little drunk, but not so much that I forgot to enact my *temblor* ritual—placing shoes, pants, and wallet by the door. Then I lay on the bed, my eyes wide open, calculating how much time it would take the next morning to make it across the city in traffic and drop off the rental car at the airport, until finally a memory arose, a benediction, guiding me toward sleep.

Once I flew into Mexico City the day before Christmas to meet Deborah, a photographer friend. We'd each booked rooms at the Majestic on the Zócalo. By early evening the downtown was nearly deserted. All of Mexico was at home with family for Christmas Eve. Traffic was scant, the sidewalks empty, the restaurants and bars closed. Even the police had turned in early. I'd never seen it so empty. We walked blocks through ghostly streets to find something to eat, feeling exposed, vulnerable, stripped of the protection of crowds. Eventually we hurried back to the hotel with a pizza.

The next morning I awoke to silence. Parting the curtains, I beheld a rare sight: the snow-tipped volcanoes Popocatépetl and Iztaccíhuatl standing sentinel over the valley. The smog had vanished, the air was sparkling and clear. Below me the vast Plaza Mayor was empty but for a lone figure or two. Over the rooftops, as far as the eye could see, Mexico City spread, crystalline and fully visible, like a great scrim or backdrop for an unsung opera.

Excitedly Deborah and I hurried out into the pristine, evacuated landscape. Crossing the abandoned Zócalo, we heard our own footsteps, stepped on our long shadows in the early orange light. As if in a dream, we walked down deserted Calle Moneda behind the National Palace, in the neighborhood of San Antonio Abad, with its great tall windows and stone walls— which had held up well in the earthquake, unlike the mostly contemporary buildings that had collapsed. "Like an Antonioni movie," Deborah said, her breathless voice echoing off the buildings in the silence. "A de Chirico painting." Deborah, drawn to ruins as backdrops for the mysterious figures in her photography, was in a rapture. As we wandered the once-grand colonial district emptied of people, it felt as if apocalypse had come and gone, wiping clean the window of time, freeing the city for an illusory moment from the torment of history. Occasional passersby couldn't help but notice each other, as if bearing the unvoiced question: *What are you doing out here? Why do you have no place to go on Christmas morning?* In this dense, foul city of human and vehicular traffic, noise, and impenetrable air that consumed, congested, and obscured—a once-green valley now verging on ecological disaster, that on the next working day, and for years of days to come, would gag on its own conquests, suffocate of its own needs and ambitions—we were allowed a hiatus, a suspension, an indrawn clear breath: a silent, holy Mexico City, innocent, unstained, and beautiful.

The next morning I set out early across the city, lurching along clogged boulevards and viaducts through spreading clouds of exhaust, sirens howling around me, grime on my lips. Locked in traffic, the minutes ticking away, coughing like a local, I felt a rising panic—*I'll never make it to the airport but simply sink into this city of mud, along with the buildings and the people in them*—until with wild relief I finally saw ahead the turnoff sign for Benito Juárez Airport.

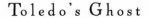

6.

Toledo's Ghost

Cloud shadows checkered the rooftops of Oaxaca City, rippled across the green valley below, scurried up the soft Sierra Madre to the east. Even before the pilot announced it, I saw, lit by a wide shaft of morning sunlight, the stone ruins of Monte Albán, supreme Zapotec ceremonial site. Its warm geometries, arrayed across the beveled mountaintop, looked mysterious and perfect. This sight alone, I thought, was worth the fifty-minute flight south from Mexico City.

As the plane settled onto the airstrip and glided to a halt before the little windsock airport, I recalled an earlier visit to Oaxaca ten years ago. I'd known I was pounding a well-worn artists' and wanderers' trail: D. H. Lawrence, Graham Greene, and Malcolm Lowry had written of it earlier, of course. ("Oaxaca," Lowry wrote in *Under the Volcano*. "The word was like a breaking heart, a sudden peal of stifled bells in a gale, the last syllables of a woman dying of thirst in the desert.") Sergei

Eisenstein, in his long-lost *Qué Viva México!*, had filmed a Oaxacan marriage ceremony—a ravished Indian bride lying on the nuptial bed in white, smothered in roses—I'd never forgotten. The region's extravagant landscapes, ancient ruins, and living indigenous cultures had inspired generations of painters, photographers, and anthropologists. In the 1960s Oaxaca was all about pilgrimages into the Sierra Masateca to visit the *bruja* María Sabena and imbibe the magic mushroom.

On that earlier visit I'd stepped off the same flight into this same subtropical air among residual hippies in graying ponytails, Mexican sandals, and faded *huipiles*, gripped by a sense that I'd landed in a place whose cultural moment had passed. The city's central plaza, the *zócalo*, with its outdoor cafés, wrought-iron benches, and costumed Indian vendors selling toasted grasshoppers beneath the drooping laurels, had seemed melancholic, the marimba orchestra in the bandstand pavilion percussing in a minor key. The small, gifted Zapotec and Mixtec geomancers who'd raised the operatic stone edifices of Monte Albán, Mitla, and Yagul—and who still made up more than half of Oaxaca City's four hundred thousand people—had appeared sullen, abstruse, under the lash of some simmering oppression. For all its wealth in history and art, Oaxaca had felt like the end of something, not a beginning. I'd left after a few days without much regret. But Masako had intimated that something new was going on in Oaxaca these days—a cultural resurgence, led by the Oaxacan artist Francisco Toledo.

Even *Time* magazine seemed to have gotten wind of it. In the Mexico City airport, looking for something to read on the plane, I'd picked up a copy of *Time*'s Latin American edition, headlined "The New Mexico." The cover image was Frida Kahlo in a Oaxacan headpiece—not Frida quite, but that same voluptuous Salma Hayek, lately of San Miguel de Allende, replete with Frida's patented run-on eyebrows, faint mustache, and signature dress, soon to star in the biopic of the tormented artist. Mexico, shouted *Time*, was spicy hot these days, with *Amores Perros* the first Mexican film to be nominated for an Academy Award. Latin pop was crawling all over the American charts. After seventy years of corrupt one-party rule, the tall, suave, English-speaking Mexican president Vicente Fox was giving Mexico a new look. A creative breakout in film, art, food, music, crafts, and architecture was taking place in cutting-edge cities like Oaxaca, *Time* breathlessly proclaimed.

The airport taxi sped past cornfields still green from summer rains. I glanced east to the mountains rimming the city, where some twenty thousand years ago descendants of migrants from Asia settled in these valleys, mountains, savannas, and tropical forests. Around 500 B.C. ruler-priests founded here what may have been America's first metropolis, Monte Albán.

"*¿De dónde viene?*" asked Rafael the *taxista*, slowing into traffic on the city outskirts.

"San Miguel de Allende," I answered, "*y* Los Angeles."

Rafael told me his nephew Julio worked in L.A. as a chef.

"What kind of food?" I asked.

"French."

We laughed. It was both a truism and a joke that in California these days, whether the food was Indian, Greek, or

Japanese, you could lay odds the chef was Mexican. Back home most Mexican men were fed and clothed by women all their life and couldn't cook a decent meal to save their souls. How did they do it?

If earlier waves of Mexican immigrants to California tended to be from central or northern Mexico—Guadalajara, Michoacán, Chihuahua—now it was often Oaxacans, descendants of these great mathematical stone builders, driven north by brutal economic conditions to find work where they could. Some opened restaurants. I told Rafael about one such Oaxacan eatery in L.A. that served rich, spicy *mole* sauces and *tlayudas*, the crackly toasted Oaxacan tortilla with lettuce, meat, tomatoes, and chiles.

"*Riquísimo,*" I said. Delicious.

"*Tal vez,*" said Rafael politely, then proceeded to rattle off a tour de force list of local dishes and ingredients, from ants to armadillos. In Oaxaca, he said, we have six hundred varieties of chiles. I thought he was going to run through the whole inventory, but he trailed off after about a dozen.

As we approached the city center, traffic slowed to let pass a demonstration of campesinos marching toward the *zócalo*, the central plaza, carrying signs protesting a new "indigenous rights" law that satisfied nobody—a reminder of who was left out of *Time*'s "New Mexico."

Rafael, garrulous fount of lore, sensing he had my interest, began telling me about *muxe*, the transsexuals of nearby Juchitán, who live as fully part of a matriarchal society. He told me how burro dung used in Oaxaca's adobe walls lasts two hundred years, and how jade had been more valuable to the Zapotecs than the gold the Spanish invaders coveted.

A few blocks past the zócalo, across from Soledad Church, we pulled up before a wrought-iron gate. Rafael, handing me his card, suggested we visit some outlying villages together or drive up to Monte Albán one day. I told him I'd call him.

The apartment was off a small courtyard—a single high room with sleeping loft, dining room, and kitchenette below. We'd sublet it for the month from a Bay Area woman I'd met, Taia, who led art classes here several times a year. I found fresh mango juice in the *refri*, as Mexicans call the refrigerator, and on the door, affixed by a magnet, a Polaroid of Taia with a handsome young Oaxacan man.

A note on the kitchen counter said: *¡Bienvenido! Off shooting rugs in Teotitlán del Valle. Back at sunset. Museum opening tonight. Love, M*

Sipping mango juice, I wriggled my way among stacks of Oaxacan rugs, shawls, and huipiles. Masako had been busy, I could see. She'd come to Oaxaca to be near the markets and surrounding villages, where traditional artisans brave the onslaught of machine-made goods with backstrap looms. A fine artist with an equally avid interest in folk arts, Masako had undertaken to write and photograph this book on Mexican textiles. I was to write the introduction; and while I'd been around her fabric passions for years, I felt poorly equipped for the job. Oaxaca, she'd assured me, was the place to fix that. Her publisher's deadline loomed; I'd need to finish my piece while I was here.

The air was growing warm in Taia's windowless flat. Eager to see more of the city, I headed out into the morning.

Walking toward the *centro* under a sharp blue October sky, I passed Internet cafés full of Oaxacan kids hunched over terminals. Kiosks hawked mobile phones. Along Calle Alcalá, the wide walk-street corridor connecting the zócalo to the great Santo Domingo Church, people seemed speedier of step these days. New handicraft shops, bookstores, galleries, and cultural centers filled the buildings along either side. This didn't feel like the torpid city I'd visited a decade earlier.

The lofty, somber cathedral of Santo Domingo, seat of the powerful Bishopric of Oaxaca that had once anchored the colonial push in the region, soared above its broad plaza. With its saints and figurines, gilt and icons, it compelled awe but not affection. True revelation lay next door, though, where the massive sixteenth-century Dominican convent, long fallen into ruin and scheduled to be turned into a shopping plaza, had been rescued and restored, due largely to the efforts of the artist Francisco Toledo. Refashioned into the Museo de las Culturas de Oaxaca by Mexico's best builders and craftsmen, this was ground zero of the "new" Oaxaca.

I wandered through light-blasted spaces, among arches and fountains and polished *cantera* stone; displays of pre-Hispanic, Spanish, and contemporary treasures; libraries and scholarly resources; treasures from the great tomb excavations at Monte Albán; a contemporary gallery. Glassless windows along the upper corridors offered views of the new botanical garden below, the city beyond, and the encircling mountains. As I emerged from this luminous, transfigured old nunnery into midday Oaxacan light, the world looked much brighter.

Across the street I entered the Instituto de Artes Gráficas de Oaxaca, gifted to the city by the artist Toledo. A pair of Odilon Redon prints hung in an old courtyard surrounded by quiet library rooms filled with students and scholars. A poster on a bulletin board listed free nightly screenings of international films at El Pochote—yet another building donated by Toledo.

Emerging back outside, I heard the words "Maestro! Maestro!" A slight, dark, long-haired, sandaled man clad in white came walking down Alcalá, accosted every few steps by a request to pose for a photo, a demand to sign a petition. I recognized him from photos as Francisco Toledo.

Born in nearby coastal Juchitán, trained in Mexico City and Paris, Toledo had gained early recognition for his charged etchings, drawings, paintings, and sculptures of insects, humans, animals, and regions of the private imagination invoking Dürer, Bosch, and the Oaxacan jungles. His reputation quickly established as the best Mexican artist of his generation, he'd returned here to live. But what he'd chosen to do with his resources was extraordinary. Extending a tradition among Oaxacan artists of plowing one's gains back into the community—knitting together, in Paz's words, the useful and the beautiful—Toledo had created, alongside Santo Domingo and the graphics workshop, an organization to help preserve the natural and cultural inheritance of Oaxaca State, a library for the blind, a photographic library, a library of recordings, and an ecological operation that manufactured art paper. Recently he'd bought an old textile factory in an adjacent hill community to house workshops for etching, photography, textiles, and design. Thanks to his efforts, UNESCO had recently declared Oaxaca City part of the cultural patrimony of humankind.

I trailed Toledo down Alcalá to the zócalo as he suffered more *saludos* and importunings. Then wishing him some peace, I veered off and took a café chair beneath the *portales*. Dipping *pan de yema*, bread with egg yolk, into hot chocolate, I watched balloon sellers drift among the crowds, listened to street guitarists croon Oaxacan classics—*"La Zandunga," "La Llorona"*—while a troupe of black-clad mariachis overlapped with a plangent *"La Vida No Vale Nada"* (Life Is Worth Nothing). This was the old Oaxaca, here at the zócalo. Equally within sight, in a corner of the square, peasant men in white cotton garments warmed tortillas and beans over a grill where they'd spent the night beneath placards appealing to the state government to bring water and electricity to their village. Further away, a group of red-costumed indigenous Triqui woman enacted a slow, turning dance mourning dead brethren at the hands of rural paramilitaries.

Beneath the arches at the far end of the plaza, a dark girl in jeans with huge eyes and straight black hair to her waist sat beneath a poster affixed to a column. It said *"Ojo por ojo / Deja el mundo ciego"* (An eye for an eye leaves the world blind)—a comment upon the U.S. invasion of Afghanistan several days earlier. A blind alto saxophone player, surely unaware of her, played a squeaky, tuneless rendition of "Misty" to my table. In Mexico, so little separates laughter from tears sometimes.

The Shit Notebooks," I said. "There's no other way to translate it."

Antonio, waving an unlit cigar, laughed. He, his wife Marietta, Masako, and I raised glasses of pale, peppery yellow *mezcal* while their two-year old, Anaïs, dashed about our feet.

"¡Salud!"

In the open courtyard of the Museo de Arte Contemporáneo that evening, we mingled among Oaxacan students, artists and collectors, and curators from Mexico City, New York, and Berlin. Upper-class Mexican matrons wore exquisite woven shawls—the same once-déclassé huipiles that indigenous women wove and wore, soon to be celebrated in Masako's book.

The occasion for the exhibition was a tax bill the Mexican government claimed Francisco Toledo owed them. When they agreed to settle for payment in artwork, Toledo, making his feelings clear, had donated a series of notebooks filled with improvisational drawings of shit: a tour de force of defecating *cucarachas* and crickets and scorpions, piles of turds bigger than people, garlands and designs of *mierda*, excreting ghosts, fecal improvisations of every possible description—playful, virtuostic, drawn with furious skill. Ironically, the government's mal-odorous gift from the artist, his *Cuadernos de la Mierda*, would smell sweeter the longer they held on to it.

Afterward we sat beneath stars in the flower-filled colonial patio of a contemporary hotel-restaurant, paintings by Oaxacan artists hanging on the whitewashed walls. I hadn't seen Toledo at the opening and wondered aloud if he was catching up on sleep, what with the endless projects that took up his time.

"Actually," Antonio said, "he's leaving Oaxaca for a year so he can get some work done."

"It's become impossible for him here," Marietta said.

"Where's he going?"

"L.A."

Of all places. I wondered if the dark artist, in his ethnic garb and sandals, walking out onto an L.A. street, would get picked up as a *pocho*, an illegal, and be deported.

Antonio, my *tocayo*—the Spanish term for two people with the same first name—was one of Mexico's best photographers. He'd shot the iconic photos the world knows of ski-masked Za-patistas marching into San Cristóbal de las Casas ten years ear-lier. Now he'd been lured from his home there to come and set up a new photography workshop in the textile factory Toledo had bought in nearby San Agostín Étla.

When Masako mentioned she was interested in going to San Cristóbal to shoot the Mayan weavers' cooperatives for her book, Antonio said, "Why don't you stay at our house?"

Food arrived, prepared by a local chef trained in France: an appetizer of pumpkin seeds, avocado, goat cheese, lime, and vinegar on tiny tostadas; then *sopa de manzana y limón* (apple and lime soup with chicken strips); and for the main course, the seasonal delicacy *chiles en nogada*, green peppers stuffed with almonds and raisins. If this was the New Oaxaca, hip and *sabroso*, I was beginning to yearn just a little for the Old Oaxaca of mole, grasshoppers, and chocolate.

Late that night Masako and I crossed the deserted compound of Soledad Church, home to Oaxaca's First Lady, the dolorous, robed Virgin of Solitude, reaching the gate to Taia's flat just as the bells tolled twelve.

It was hot in the sleeping loft, with no window or skylight to let out the day's air. We'd planned to get up early and go to the outlying markets and villages, but it was late now, and setting an alarm seemed brutal. We lay surrounded by photos of Taia and the boyfriend on the walls, the bureau, the table— romantic images, holding up a slightly poignant mirror to our long marriage.

It was the first time we'd been alone since I'd arrived. We traded news of family in California. I caught her up on doings in San Miguel—house, friends, life along Calle Flor, and the movie crew that had taken over the town; my visit to the Sierra Gorda and my strange encounters there; my stopover in Mexico City. She talked enthusiastically about her progress with the book, the stimulation of life in Oaxaca, and new friends she wanted me to meet.

"I can see why you like it here," I said. Oaxaca was a visual feast, an artist's town devoted to her twin passions, serious contemporary art and ethnic crafts. "Could you live here?"

"Rents aren't bad. Houses are expensive to buy." She looked at me. "If we were starting over in Mexico, I think I might prefer it."

What binds, what dissolves? What sunders, what holds? After all these years, if we could each do exactly what we wanted, would our desires still match? Writing and art-making were privileged professions, if fragile and uncertain. Masako seemed content for now in Oaxaca, as I was elsewhere these days. In theory we could work anywhere—and work was what we both did, relentlessly. But art depended upon inspiration, after all, and finding the right place was part of that. Once years ago we'd asked these same questions of ourselves and found an answer, together, in San Miguel de Allende.

When Masako had fallen asleep, I took from Taia's bedstand an old copy of Lowry's *Under the Volcano*. By a tiny lamp, I read: "But it was as though their love were wandering over some desolate cactus plain, far from here, lost, stumbling and falling, attacked by wild beasts, calling for help—dying, to sigh at last, with a kind of weary peace: Oaxaca."

7.

Techno Tribal

The next day, and in days to follow, Masako and I crossed and recrossed Oaxaca's bright Valle de Tlacolula, visiting villages and bazaars, bending over displays of folk art at Ocotlán's sprawling Friday market, sitting with the rug-weaving families of Teotitlán del Valle, crouched on blankets among the sellers at the Tlacolula market while Masako gathered samples or shot with her Canon EOS. Back in Oaxaca City we haunted off-street markets, crafts centers, and solo artisans' workshops, sifting a cornucopia of regional riches—handwoven fabrics, masks, baskets, pottery, and handmade papers of maguey or banana leaf made at one of Toledo's new workshops.

One morning, trailing Masako into the tumult of the covered Juárez market, just south of the zócalo, I heard *"Mezcal, mi amor?"*

I turned to smile at the teenage seller's whispered enticement to sample her display of agave liquors. When I turned back around, Masako was gone. A pulsing synesthesia of smells, sounds, and sights carried me past sellers of wooden combs, leather sandals, *rebozos*, costume jewelry, fresh flowers, and shrines to favored saints. A marimba band punched a knobby *"Malagueña"* into the fragrant air. Strolling women proffered bowls of edible worms (four different kinds, sold live and writhing or in a succulent sauce), wasps, grasshoppers, and ants. Hopelessly lost, I ended up in a shop called Chocolate Mayordomo, watching young men measure and grind local *moles* and chocolates in great metal vats, mixing in cacao, almonds, or sugar to taste. I didn't catch up to Masako until that evening at Taia's flat.

At Amate Books on Calle Alcalá, with its keen selection of titles in Spanish and English, we met up one afternoon with the owner and Oaxaca veteran Henry Wangeman, and the three of us headed off for lunch at Yu Ne Hisa (Earth and Water, in Zapotec), a simple eatery featuring food from the coastal town of Juchitán. We'd come for the iguana soup (in which head and tail are served as garni), but the genial *dueña*, in her Tehuana garb (like Frida, like Salma), was out of it, so we settled for her *mole de camarones* (shrimp soup à la Juchitán) and armadillo stew (with one claw sticking up from the meat!), and we did not complain.

Afterward we drifted through the Museo Arte Prehispánico de Rufino Tamayo, where the earlier Oaxacan master painter's vast, whimsical collection of preclassical figurines and artifacts—witty, emotive, anthropomorphic—seemed to forge another link to that vibrant ruined world on the plateau I'd seen from the arriving plane. This little museum, once Tamayo's house, existed only because Francisco Toledo had secured support to keep it going.

The next afternoon we arrived at the house of the Oaxacan artist Laura Hernández for lunch at two-thirty. Nobody was there yet, and Laura was still upstairs getting ready. Too late, we realized we'd veered off Mexican time. Eventually guests from a dozen different countries began arriving, and *comida* (lunch), eventually served around five, ran deep into the night. Homemade moles and tamales filled plates, music played, and conversation flowed in Spanish, Zapotec, English, French, and German. We watched a video of a film made for German television on the Oaxacan–North American singer Lila Downs, her rich vocalizations and transmuted renditions of indigenous songs soon to be featured in Salma Hayek's *Frida*. The film's director, who was at the lunch, had returned to Oaxaca to make a film on our hostess, Laura, a beautiful *oaxaqueña* who dressed in clothes from Tehuantapec (like Frida, like Salma, like the proprietess of Yu Ne Hisa), had studios in Mexico City and Amsterdam, and exhibited her paintings all over the world.

Exhilarating days, woven through contemporary and ancient Oaxaca; rich evenings, at dinners or exhibitions among new friends or simply by ourselves—always ending back at Taia's little flat across from Soledad Church, alone with each other, and the work that drove us, our uncertain futures arrayed about us like the growing piles of fabric samples Masako collected.

Late one morning, in a light drizzle, I drove out to nearby San Agostín Étla with Antonio the photographer. We climbed the muddy path to the old textile mill, among construction workers and paper makers already installed in their workshop. Antonio, at Francisco Toledo's invitation, had moved from his home in Chiapas to set up and teach a photo workshop at San Agostín; he and Marietta had just bought a house in the foothills close by.

"Toledo's presence in Oaxaca has changed everything," Antonio said on the drive back. "It's a total culture he's supporting, a sensibility. Not just art but music, theater, cultural history, programs for kids. He's created a sense of the entire city as a museum."

Toledo seemed an exemplar, a beacon—a man on another path entirely, creating where others were wont to tear down. I tried to think of an American or European artist of his stature who had taken on such a role but couldn't. Can art speak to power? Images and words seemed such pitiable responses to the world's pain sometimes; yet in the nearly two months since the September 11 attacks, I'd noticed it was often poems people e-mailed each other.

"It's ironic," I said, "that Toledo has to flee to get his own work done."

"Sure. But he knows the situation he has created will survive without him now. And he'll return."

Back in the city, Antonio and I stopped at the Centro Fotográfico Bravo, which housed an exhibition and study space for contemporary photography dedicated to Mexico's first great photographer, Oaxacan Manuel Alvárez Bravo. Arrayed around a modest courtyard in a restored colonial building, it deployed the sparest of materials: rare native cacti set against deep red earthen walls, a simple stone canal bisecting the terra-cotta patio floor, old beams and arches set in white interior walls. This small space, with its quiet amalgam of ancient and new, seemed to capture the deep, invigorating cultural sense I was finding at every turn in Oaxaca.

How's your introduction coming?" Masako asked one morning.

We were sitting in Taia's loft, sipping coffee and eating homemade carrot bread we'd found in a little *puesto* behind Soledad Church. Photos and samples and text pages lay arrayed about us like so much footage. Our month at Taia's flat was nearing its end. Soon Masako would be heading north to meet with her publisher and visit her family in San Francisco. I'd be wending a path back through San Miguel before joining her in California for Christmas.

"Something still bothers me," I said.

In traditional indigenous culture, as I understood it, garments passed from generation to generation, within families and tribes. Clothing was emblematic of identity. Design motifs were developed from perceptions of self and mythologies of the natural world. Now women, sometimes also men, wove not for themselves but for the market. If the cultural context of weaving is dying, or dead, is this merely a mercantile transaction? Are these gorgeous clothes being bought literally off these weaving women's backs? Would these textile artisans—whose sons I saw hunched over computer terminals in the city, leaving tribal confines to enter the greater world through cyberspace—be better off learning contemporary skills? I needed to be clear about this, I said, to finish the introduction to her book.

Masako had been here in July, when native groups from throughout the state descend upon Oaxaca for the week-long folkloric festival of Guelaguetza. Indian dialects spice the air; Spanish is a second language if spoken at all. A queen is chosen—not the most conventionally beautiful woman, but the one who most artfully represents her village and its traditions in dress and speech. It was soul-stirring, she said, to hear these women declaim with pride and force of their origins and traditions and assert the value they place on their customs and arts; to watch them parade through the streets in their stunning costumes.

"Believe me, their identities are intact," she said. "Besides, they keep the best huipiles for themselves."

If, in the end, a woman in a New York City boutique comes upon an exquisite handwoven Mexican textile, dyed a subtle red from the insect cochineal, imagining it as a table runner for her dining room, or as a hanging for her bedroom wall, and decides to purchase it, both weaver and buyer are doing more than collaborating in supporting an ancient, living culture, Masako said. They are exchanging a recognition—of art, of pleasure, of beauty.

An eye for an eye: revealing, not blinding. I thought of the long-haired girl I passed every day in the zócalo sitting beneath her poster of protest.

Zapotec, Amuzgo, Maya, and other peoples of Oaxaca and Chiapas often weave the horizontal diamond shape. The diamond's four points represent the cardinal directions. The center is a window or door to the universe. In some garments the diamond rests over the chest area, signifying the center of the universe: here, where the wearer is. When the wearer dies, her soul exits through that door.

The next night we boarded a ten-thirty overnight bus for Chiapas, hoping to find there the final elements for her book. A dark, sinuous mountain descent landed us in the warm Pacific coast town of Juchitán, where we ate tamales at the bus station in the middle of the night. On the twisting, bilious dawn ride up switchbacks into high jungle, I gave up the tamale in the bus bathroom. Arriving in San Cristóbal de las Casas, we heard that masked Zapatista insurgents had barricaded the road we'd entered by just after we'd passed, allowing no more passage in or out of the city.

We found Antonio's home on the edge of town—a two-story house, set against a hillside, with a vegetable garden and a studio. It was a half-hour walk to the center by way of roads patrolled by street dogs. Since I'd last been in San Cristóbal in 1993, months before the invasion of indigenous guerrillas calling themselves Zapatistas, the city had become, paradoxically, more affluent and modern. After the uprising the rebels had retreated to the jungle where they remained, embodying a permanent grievance. Mexican social programs, along with thousands of soldiers, had been thrown into the region as a balm, as if to instantly redress 450 years of needs unmet. Young Europeans especially, lured by the town's smoky beauty and the radical chic of the Zapatistas' Subcomandante Marcos—whose ski-masked representation on little woven dolls lined the streets—had flocked to the moody highland city, some staying on to open cafés, boutiques, and trekking services. ATM machines, cyber-cafés, and bed-and-breakfasts dotted the downtown blocks. At Na Balom—the hacienda where the Danish anthropologist Franz Blom and his Austrian photographer wife Trudy had once hosted earlier generations of authors and explorers—a New Age staff offered pricey rooms. The walls were hung with photos of the Lacondon Indians of the mahogany forests, whom the Bloms had sheltered and labored to save, now nearly extinct from alcohol and development.

In nearby San Juan Chamula the village church still resembled a native temple, festooned with indigenous motifs and bright-colored streamers. Inside there were no pews, the floors strewn with green hay, Coke bottles, and clusters of white candles. The chant of kneeling Chamulans in woven costumes—*Nananananananana . . .*—sounded more like the guttural invocations of Tibetan monks than anything remotely Catholic.

I watched the weaving women emerge out of the dawn mist, padding down the highland roads into San Cristóbal.

Small, dark, and beautiful, they glided over the cobbled streets barefoot, piles of fabric balanced on their heads, the intense colors of their huipiles set against the old colonial buildings. Some had children on their backs, swaddled in the garment called *tzute*. Taking their places in the plazas and markets as morning sun broke through the mist, they laughed and teased, at ease with one another, like sisters. They looked indomitable, these weaving women of Chiapas, their gazes sharp and unafraid, their smiles eternal, defiant.

At a weavers' cooperative set in a cloister of the ex-convent Santo Domingo, I watched a brightly garbed Mayan weaver run a Mexican customer's Visa card through a machine, talk to her in Spanish, then resume her conversation in Tzotzil with her costumed colleague. While Masako talked with a weaver at her loom and took photos, I sat outside on a low wall among a group of Chamulan women, their wares spread on blankets, writing the last part of my introduction:

In ways we can't always describe, we mourn the loss of art and sensuousness in a utilitarian world. The more technology invades our lives, with its flood of impersonal, colorless, and "branded" objects, the more value we find in a handwoven Mexican cloth dyed from indigo, sea snails, cochineal, mosses, or tree bark. A serape come upon in a Mexican market, or in a shop where one lives, brings aesthetics back into our life: color, pattern, texture. Time slows down, if only for a moment, releasing us from harried, hurried lives; for it takes a long time to weave, and the result is something that only time can deliver.

Woven objects connect us to our own vanished histories; after all, who among us cannot trace our origins back to ancestors who wove? Handwoven textiles sustain and advance a living culture for both maker and user. Further, they propose an alternative conversation between industrial and preindustrial societies in place of the weapons-driven one presently engulfing us.

The mountain road connecting San Cristóbal to the rest of Mexico remained blocked by the Zapatistas. We waited it out at Antonio's until they'd retreated back into the jungle, then boarded a morning bus for the twelve-hour ride back to Oaxaca. In the Tuxtla Gutiérez station, armed immigration agents boarded the bus and snatched two young men sitting across from us—Guatemalans who'd sneaked across the border, surely hoping to make it all the way north to find jobs in Los Estados.

During our last days in Oaxaca City, we stayed on successive nights in four different hotels I thought I should investigate for the magazine. Clearly Oaxaca had to figure in any piece on what was new or exciting in Mexico today. This hotel-hopping was a kind of subsidized sport, a heady release from the confines of Taia's, even if studying luxury isn't the same as simply enjoying it. Artful, serene Casa Oaxaca, where we'd eaten with Antonio and Marietta and Anaïs my first night here, offered stylish contemporary rooms in the midst of the city. The equestrian appointments of a rambling ex-hacienda at the northern edge of the city seemed sterile after the festive centro. Back in town, we bedded for a night among the great stone precincts of Camino Real Oaxaca, the former convent of Santa Catalina de Siena, built in 1576, and the next morning feasted on a voluminous breakfast buffet to a soundtrack of chanting monks. Our last night in Oaxaca we spent at Las Bugambilias, a hospitable inn run by Oaxacan friends Emilia Arroyo and her family, filled with folk art and served by her natural foods restaurant.

The next morning over breakfast Masako said, "I've been offered a show at Toledo's gallery, Quetzalli, next year. There's a little place near Taia's, a sublet for two hundred dollars a month. When the book is done I think I'd like to come back, spend more time here."

"I can't think of a better place," I said.

So back to our separate adventures. Excited for ourselves, for each other. Once again it would be *adiós, nos vemos* for a while. Running in parallel more than together these days, shadowed by unvoiced prospects. Separations didn't frighten us. We understood what it meant to miss each other. But were displacement and distance becoming steady states?

Rafael, the scholarly taxista, pulled up the winding mountain road, regaling us with Zapotec, Nahuatl, and Spanish names of things, cures, and customs: *chichicastli,* a poisonous vine also used as a curative by *brujas* but deadly if not used in the right proportions; *chamiso*, another local plant, good for the stomach; the spindly tree growing by the roadside called *casahuate*, its huge fluffy white flowers (they look like gathered handkerchiefs) called *pájaro bobo* (twitty bird, or silly bird).

It was already dusk when we entered the vast arena of Monte Albán. Masako's plane to Mexico City would leave in a few hours. Crossing the wide, leveled expanse, we mounted the stone stairs of the Northern Platform, then turned and stood, gazing back across the main plaza—a thousand yards long, two-thirds as wide—at pyramids and platforms, inscriptions and murals, tombs and observatories. Built two and a half millennia ago without the aid of wheels, horses, mules, or oxen, Monte Albán served as cultural and religious center to as many as forty thousand people until around A.D. 1000, when it was mysteriously abandoned.

Silence, grandeur: mirror of earth and sky. Shadows advanced up the stone steps toward us. A crescent moon hung, like a sliver of doubt, in the darkening sky. Far below us the lights of the city winked on. Across the valley of Oaxaca, the fierce cultural energy of those early city builders survived—in painting, sculpture, ceramics, music, weaving—a tapestry of artisanship running from Francisco Toledo back to this core site, Monte Albán: silent witness to conquest and collapse, death and renewal, all that separates and unites.

8.

Dinner with Lauren

Early that November, after my weeks in Oaxaca and Chiapas, I made a series of short trips in and around Mexico City. It was hard to discern, in bustling, smoggy Cuernavaca, an hour distant from the capital, the quiet town under the volcano that had drawn writers, artists, and eccentrics of an earlier era. In nearby Tepotzlán, birthplace of the Aztec serpent-god Quetzalcoatl, proto-hippies selling crystals and tie-dyed T-shirts in the plaza seemed to have commandeered the erstwhile midcentury artists' bohemia. In Valle de Bravo, a popular pine-forested retreat to the north, noise from the boats on the artificial lake, cheesy tourist kiosks along the old cobbled streets, and traffic jams on the road out infected the beauty of the setting. The pressures of the swelling capital had tainted its old getaways, it seemed; after resonant Oaxaca, they felt tinny.

From the window of a Flecha Amarilla bus running north to San Miguel, I gazed out at burning husks of maize, black

crows wheeling over fields. Verdant when I traveled this road a
month earlier, the earth was brown now, the air dry. November
is a time of special feeling in Mexico, the country's rich relationship to the subject of mortality coming to the fore. All over
Mexico a curiously festive dance of death takes place. On the
second day of the month, cemeteries throughout the country fill
with visitors for Day of the Dead. In the city of Guanajuato, the
plazas brim with *puestos*, stalls, sporting thousands of the most
astounding handmade *alfeñiques*, little sugar or chocolate objects, often in the form of skulls, some with personalized
names—also animals, cars, houses, practically anything one
could imagine. In homes and public buildings, altars are
erected: tall tables with four wands on each corner, candles, incense, photographs of the deceased—and a profusion of rich
gold *cempasuchi*, the "flower of four hundred petals" that we call
marigold. In that November of 2001, surely a year of death, I'd
seen such an altar erected in Mexico City's Tepito Market in
memory of a young man immolated in the World Trade Center
attacks, his earnest young eyes gazing out from what looked to
be a graduation snapshot.

The landscape outside the bus window mutated from city
to suburb to fields of corn, burros, shepherds, and hooded
women in *rebozos*: traveling back in time. I'd chosen a second-
class bus over the big, new direct *primera clases* with their
booming television monitors, hoping to allow a dream corridor
of transition to unfold at the window—as it had on that first
Mexican bus ride to San Miguel sixteen years earlier, altering
my course forever.

Hilario and I stood in the rear garden of the house on Calle Flor, looking at Clorox bottles, sponges, and tissues strewn among the irises and agapanthas. The maid at the new bed and breakfast next door was dumping, or letting fall, her refuse from two stories above. This meant I'd have to go talk to the neighbor while I was here, which I didn't fancy; we'd already had a dispute about our common wall, which she was obliged to paint but hadn't. Hilario, steeped in town gossip, confided that the señora allegedly owed money around town. A bad sort, we agreed. He pointed out that the chirimoya tree was shedding leaves that had to be cleaned and hauled away. The jacaranda was growing too fast, spreading its roots under the house. There seemed to be a leak in the gas line, requiring the services of Alfredo the plumber. Householder talk. I had a hard time connecting. I was still on the road, in buses and cars and planes and strange towns, in the grips of my "dissociative fugue," which I'd lately come to think of with a certain *ternura*, a tenderness.

Dusk fell early in the garden since the new wall went up next door. In the front patio, where there was still light, we talked about the new candidates for mayor, the unseasonably warm early winter, his family. Miguel, his oldest son, an engineer at a U.S. firm in Querétaro, had a brand-new car and was engaged to be married. The next three sons ran Internet cafés around town, repaired computers, and built websites. From their modest house in the Azteca neighborhood, his ten kids were leaving home, one by one, entering the professional class and with it the greater world, leaving Hilario scratching his head in confusion and not a little pride.

In the dining room we moved a heavy table away from the yard-thick adobe wall to examine water damage along the base. Huffing, we lifted the table back into place, looked at each other, and laughed. Years had passed; neither of us was getting any younger. We used to lug huge beds and armoires around and in fact still did, though we probably shouldn't. Hilario, too macho to wear glasses, let me read the water meter by the front door; then he stood far back, squinting, to eye a screw before attacking it with his *atornillador*.

I opened the old door in the wall dividing our house from the casita, where James, our writer friend, had been staying. He'd returned to the States for the holidays, as would I too before long. Inside I could feel the chill through the casita walls and the floor tiles. Time to lay in some *leña*, firewood. Early December days in these mountains were still warm and sunny, if short, but the nights could be nippy. Soon our brief winter would send howling winds to strip the gardens of their blooms, freeze citrus trees in the *campo*—and on the steps of the Parroquia, free blankets would be handed out to the *pobres*.

When I came back outside, Hilario was gone. I went to our bedroom, threw on a jacket, and headed out into the evening.

Shutting the front door behind me, I heard a voice say, in English, "Hold it right there."

A camera went off.

"Thanks. Loved your book."

Across the street, a figure dashed off. Reactively, I muttered after him an unheard "Thank you."

I stood in the twilight, feeling vaguely assaulted. A book I'd written about our life here had incited a gamut of local reactions, from pleasure that someone had finally gotten the place right to accusations that I'd despoiled the town—though this seemed a silly charge, as San Miguel had been appearing on travel magazines' top-ten lists for some years. A few people had thought they recognized themselves in the book and reacted with either irritation or vanity, which had taken a while to settle out. I used to skulk around the town unshaven; now I never knew when a friendly stranger would ambush me with chat or a camera or a book to sign. Some days I'd answer a knock on my door to find someone unknown to me wanting to come in and look around my house, as if it were some sort of museum and not the place where we lived and worked. Still, I knew I was part of the problem I decried—I'd written about that too—and could hardly blame anyone but myself. As a friend had put it bluntly one evening at El Petit Bar, "This is what happens when you shit in your own backyard."

Gradually things had calmed down, the book becoming just another artifact of town lore. New scandals had emerged to take center stage, most recently the invasion of *Once Upon a Time in Mexico*, whose cast and crew had decamped at last. Now we had only to await the supercharged, star-soaked result in cineplexes, see our little jardín on the big screen, hear the Parroquia's bells in Dolby SurroundSound. But as I walked up deserted Calle Flor in the early evening, the aroma of burning mesquite from winter fires sweetening the air, it felt like San Miguel had been returned, for the moment at least, to its residents.

I found my old friend Lauren sitting on a bench in front of the Parroquia, wrapped in a shawl. The holiday season was gearing up in earnest, with twelve days of *posadas* and *pastorelas* to be got through before Christmas Day, then further festivities until Three Kings Day, January 6. No holiday goes unremarked or uncelebrated in San Miguel, and workmen were already stringing Christmas lights in the jardín's laurel trees, fencing off and laying hay in the little manger below the pavilion that would house the Madonna-and-child crèche, the little live lambs and calves. In the *portales* a mariachi troupe was serenading an image of that other beloved virgin, the indigenous Guadalupe, mother of all Mexico, whose birthday was that very day, the twelfth of December.

As I sat down beside Lauren, a great clanging erupted from the Parroquia bell tower. Members of a large Saturday wedding party emerged from the church and spilled into the plaza, the priest parting the guests like water to bless the honeymoon car. A blinkered dray horse stood indifferently nearby, two girls in *playeras*, T-shirts, selling ice cream from metal tubs off the haywagon in back. Roaming balloon sellers punctuated the view of a bullfight poster announcing the next afternoon's attractions—among them La Güerita, a blond lady sensation from Texas who had been gored the Sunday before in Mexico City "in the groin area," according to this morning's *El Sol de Bajío*.

When a rock band began to unhouse its instruments on a riser beneath the bell tower, threatening to push the *alegría* beyond the endurable, I said to Lauren, "So where shall we eat?"

"The Ambos Mundos," she answered quickly.

An interesting choice. Both of us had begun our very different San Miguel lives there.

Our route took us past the huge compound of the ex-nunnery, Las Monjas, now the Bellas Artes Institute. Posters in the foyer announced winter classes in various plastic arts, a round of chamber music concerts, the upcoming annual January poetry workshops, and a series of literary lectures put on by the local branch of PEN, the international writers' group. An arty little town indeed, and a lively agenda for the snowbirds from the north soon to descend upon the town. Inside, a reception was in progress for an artist whose work Lauren knew and thought we could safely skip.

A little further on we paused before the high, vine-thronged entry of the Hotel Ambos Mundos, registering whatever emotions it might evoke in each of us.

"*Recuerdos,*" Lauren said, sighing. Memories.

Federico had made a fire inside, as it was too cold to eat on the patio. One other table was occupied with what appeared to be a Mexico City couple. We took a seat halfway between the fireplace and the door, beneath the posters of Italy and the empty liquor bottles along the ledge. *"Tequilitas?"* Federico called from behind the bar.

Lauren took off her shawl and put it with her purse on an empty chair. "Federico must have come here around the same time we did."

"He probably started out from a room at the Ambos Mundos too."

"A rambling ex-hacienda full of characters for four dollars a night. It was hard to beat."

From our table I could see across the hotel entrada into the office where Rafael the proprietor sat behind the reception desk, exactly as he had so many years ago, looking up at the television in the same pale windbreaker, nervously tapping his foot.

"Old Emil the painter," Lauren said, "sitting here gumming *frijoles*, talking about his pal Henry Miller."

"Comida was sixty-five cents. For some reason that number sticks in my head."

"The hotels were empty. You could just go swim in their pools. Mexico seemed almost a forgotten place then."

"The earlier generation of Mexicophiles had moved on," I said. "The peso had collapsed. Then the earthquake hit."

"Things were harder to come by. Books, food, news. It gave life a piquancy, a preciousness."

Lauren was a writer of short stories and a translator, a good one. She'd come here from New York with her little girl, Celia, after her marriage to an editor had broken up. She would have been about thirty then, tall and raven-haired and quite beautiful. She'd lived in the capital for a while, then moved here. Celia had grown up in San Miguel, smart and bilingual, and had a handsome Cuban boyfriend named Luis. This fall she'd headed off to NYU to study film.

"I remember deep, hungry exchanges with Mexican friends," Lauren said. "People would give letters to departing gringos to mail. Yesterday on Calle San Francisco I sent a package to Celia in New York that will arrive tomorrow morning."

Federico, cigarette dangling from his mouth, sent our tequilas by way of the waiter with a high sign. A number of Italians had arrived in San Miguel when we did, finding their way into different corners of the town, opening coffee bars and restaurants. With a Mexican wife, a little daughter, and his trattoria, Federico had grown portly and content, it seemed. The food had never been great here—his ex-partner Alberto, who could actually cook, had served far better cuisine at his restaurant across town until he allegedly impregnated one of his kitchen workers and his wife had given him the boot and taken over. But the menu here improved every summer when Federico's mother came to visit from Cremona. And the Ambos Mundos courtyard, and this soaring interior dining room, offered a rich *ambiente*.

"I remember when Banamex's ATM machine appeared one morning in the *portales*," I said. "It felt as if a wall had been breached—the end of something and the beginning of something else."

"Sometimes I think it would be better to be either farther away or closer in," Lauren said. "At the center or at the edges. Not in some globalized expatriate limbo."

Expatriate. The term sounded dated. Nowadays people lived where they lived, whether it was in their home country or another, for any of a thousand reasons. MTV played in coffee shops in Burma, the Internet was a spaceless world, and *Lonely Planet* had mapped every turn in the road. Crossing a border was crossing town. Did expatriates even exist anymore?

"On the plane from Oaxaca to Mexico City," I said, "I saw an ad in a magazine. A man in a bathing suit was floating on a lagoon in a rubber raft on some remote tropical island, a mobile phone to his ear. It said, 'With AT&T'—or whichever company it was—'you'll never be out of touch!' "

"That's just it," Lauren said. "It's getting hard to be out of touch. But it's sometimes in silence, distance, strangeness— things we found here—that revelation and understanding come."

We exchanged *saluds*, then noted a few passings. Stirling Dickenson, San Miguel's founding gringo, as he was thought of with considerable affection, had died at ninety-two when he'd backed his car off a road into a ravine. Fernando Maqueo, a gentle poet we'd both been fond of, had died unexpectedly; homages had appeared in the local papers.

"Things have quieted down since the film crew cleared out," Lauren said, "though I have to say it was nice book-browsing next to Johnny Depp at El Tecolote."

I'd picked up the menu and begun to read when Lauren said suddenly, "Tony, I'm leaving."

I looked at her in utter surprise—both at the news and at the sense of loss it stirred in me. In a small town, people want confirmation that this is still the good place, that their choice is holding up. Defections are noted. When a cultured, accomplished friend departs, the loss is all the greater.

I was sure she had her reasons. When she'd first come here, it was the heyday of the Latin American authors she translated. Lauren had found in Mexico a renewed Catholicism and a personal relationship to the Virgin Mary. Now San Miguel was changing, suffering an invasion of people quite different from the earlier arrivals. Mexican and foreign communities were drawing apart. A recent romance with Juan Carlos, a self-styled composer and local roué, had ended badly. Her daughter was gone, and she was alone.

"I can live quite happily by myself," she said. "It's not that. Sure, the town isn't the same, but enough of the old remains, and some people I love. Mexico surrounds us. It's just that . . . well, we've lived through a cycle of discovery here." She reached for her menu. "I see you bouncing off the walls a little too, no?"

After we'd ordered pasta and *vino tinto*, Lauren took a deep breath and continued:

"In September Celia was out of the city—thank God— when the World Trade Center attack happened. When she got back to her highrise downtown, she found the plate glass window shattered, debris everywhere." Lauren's eyes filled with tears. "She sits in her friend's flat, trembling. She can't concentrate, go to courses. She can't bear to return to her apartment." She downed her tequila. "I have to go back."

What yokes us to a place? A country not one's own by birth, or upbringing, or language, will always be an imagined landscape, a borrowed landscape, in a way. Of course that's its very attraction. Even among adventurous souls like Lauren, who would always choose freedom over belonging, in the end it was often blood, family that drew them back.

"A tough time to be returning to New York," I said.

Two musicians we knew entered with their instrument cases and set them down by the bar. Gil, a guitarist from Oaxaca, and Cartas, a defected Cuban violinist, had arrived in San Miguel around the same time as we had, forming a duo that had since taken them all over Latin America.

"I thought I'd found a fixed spot on the compass," Lauren said. "Maybe that's asking too much of any one place."

I heard the defeat in her voice, still only half-believing she was serious about leaving.

She raised her wineglass. "To El Vigilante."

Not long ago letters had begun appearing in San Miguel mailboxes, written in Spanish and English, signed "El Vigilante." The writer's complaint was that the arrival of ever more foreigners was driving up prices in San Miguel, robbing Mexico of its patrimony. El Vigilante's screeds denouncing the gringo presence provided uneasy amusement around local dinner tables; after all, they bore an honest, if discomfiting, measure of truth. But when he began threatening to write the IRS in Washington, naming names of people who had bought houses and had bank accounts here, the tolerant foreign smiles disappeared. Among Mexicans I'd spoken to, he'd hit a raw nerve and was gaining support: they had a growing list of resentments toward the new arrivals especially, many of whom didn't bother to learn Spanish or integrate into the community. I found El Vigilante's letters great reading, though his xenophobia seemed a little misplaced to me, coming as I did from California, host to millions of Mexicans, most undocumented—not just workers but very rich ones who had plowed their often ill-gotten Mexican gains into mansions all over La Jolla, San Diego, Palos Verdes, and Santa Barbara. I cringed at some of my fellow citizens' rude habits here in Mexico, but how threatening in a country of a hundred million people were a few thousand gringos who paid their way?

Then it was revealed by someone who knew El Vigilante that he was from Mexico City, not San Miguel—and worse, he wasn't Mexican at all but a Spaniard, one of those archcolonizers Mexico had launched a revolution to drive out! Exactly why the letters stopped coming or how the man was booted, or eased, out of town was unknown to me but not hard to guess. City officials, we figured, who were doing quite well off the foreign presence, had let El Vigilante know, *en la manera mexicana*, that he was no longer welcome here.

The restaurant had filled up around us. Gil and Cartas were tuning up. Our voices rose a notch to keep pace.

"You seem to have quite a wanderlust these days," Lauren said. "Where are you off to next?"

Wanderlust. How much simpler, more descriptive a term than *dissociative fugue*—admitting the notion of desire, not just involuntary compulsion framed in the jargon of a medical diagnosis.

"Guanajuato," I said. "Then California for Christmas. In January Veracruz, the Yucatán. Some friends are making a film on Mayan temple inscriptions. I'll join them in southern Mexico for some days. I'll have a magazine piece to finish up. Then possibly a trip to Chile, Bolivia, Peru next year."

"Send postcards, will you?"

"I promise."

Gil and Cartas launched into "Limehouse Blues," drowning out the possibility of further conversation. Lauren wrote out the address of Celia's apartment where she'd be staying until she got settled. I raised my arm and scribbled on the air to signal Federico for the check.

Outside, without really deciding it, we turned away from the entrance and walked deeper into the grounds of the Ambos Mundos. The night had warmed a little. A half moon hung over the huge orange tree in the courtyard. Passing Rafael's paired parrots in their cages, Lauren said, "I know parrots live a long time, but these can't be the same ones that were here when we were."

"Rafael still wears the same windbreaker."

"He should treat himself to a new one. They're making money now."

We passed Lauren's old room, one of the few with a fireplace, as I remembered. Seeing a light on behind its curtain, an image arose of the man who had moved in after Lauren left.

A heavy summer rain had settled in that year. I recalled the flare of a match, the orange tip of a cigarette, the silhouette of another storm-stranded boarder hovering in the gloom in front of his door. Reverend Billy, as he called himself, was a large, bespectacled man, some manner of defrocked evangelical who had harvested souls in Asia, Africa, and Latin America, then become ensnared in his own nets—a messy descent entailing women, unsavory politics, and that unholy cocktail, amphetamines and drink. He appeared to be a military intelligence floater of some lower rank as well, with roots going back to the Bay of Pigs debacle—though the shiny-eyed, unctuous preacher liked to describe himself as simply a widower enjoying cheap lodgings and the local AA chapter in San Miguel. He'd look at you sideways to see if you believed him, not really caring if you did.

His clandestine style did border on the comic: "Say, what do the civilians call the currency around here?" Reverend Billy didn't kill a cockroach, he "terminated" it. Before leaving his room he "deactivated" his light switch. He ate "rations" at "twenty hundred hours," not dinner at eight like the rest of us.

Reverend Billy was a source of considerable amusement and speculation around the Ambos Mundos. But I remember once coming up behind him in the *mercado* and tapping his shoulder. He'd spun around, karate hands up, ready to "take me out," as he'd put it. It had scared the hell out of me.

My room was across the courtyard from his, and sometimes I used to watch Reverend Billy standing under the eaves in the rain, looking off into the ghostly dripping jacarandas, drawing on his smoke, and I'd wonder what the old fisher of souls was thinking.

Then one weekend Reverend Billy fell off the wagon. For days he lay around his room at the Ambos Mundos in his undershirt, drinking boilermakers. He said he was going south to "visit the ruins at Tikal" when the weather let up. As if he cared about archaeology. My guess was he'd been reactivated and was about to go kick up some unrepentant dust in Managua or maybe Salvador, for the contra wars were still in progress. Passing his room on the way to my own, I'd see him through the slightly parted curtain, lying on the bed with his drink and his Camels, conducting some tortured colloquium with the air. I wanted to think what was bothering him was a belated encounter with that very conscience from which he had become estranged somewhere along the way, though this seemed overly hopeful.

The last time I saw Reverend Billy, I was hurrying back to my room in the rain when he emerged out of the gloom and grabbed my arm. I could smell the rum and sweat on him. He fixed his oily regard upon me and said, "Sinners all, young man. Here but to serve His inscrutable ends." Licking his lips, he said, "God bless, God bless." Then flicking his Camel into the rain, he pulled his slicker up around him like a shroud and stumbled off across the courtyard.

The next morning the rain had let up. A bright, blasting sun dried the courtyard cobbles as I watched. I saw a bucket and mop outside Reverend Billy's room. Irma, one of the girls who cleaned at the hotel, was inside, clearing out the stinking strew of empty bottles and crumpled Camel packs. Reverend Billy was gone.

Now passing the room that had been his, and Lauren's before him, I found myself wondering where Reverend Billy was today. Kabul? Damascus? Mosul? Mucking things up, as he probably had in Phnom Penh, Santiago, Managua?

Lauren and I, following a gravel path past a row of rooms that had once been stables, came to the scrambled, untended rear garden, hung with hotel washing. The long swimming pool, barely lit from a nearby room, was still cracked, still empty.

"We used to call that pool the Mosquito Farm," Lauren said. "There was a guy who'd always sit here sunning himself behind dark glasses. He developed a rather obsessive interest in me."

"Mad Julian?"

"Oh, God. He's why I moved out."

"I think he was repatriated in the end. Back to St. Louis or somewhere."

At the far end of the path, a man was sitting alone in the dark, hunched over a little wooden table lit only by a candle.

"Buenas noches."

As we drew closer, I saw a grizzled gringo in a serape and a sombrero, a collection of empty beer bottles arrayed before him, and a pack of Faros, the cheap Mexican cigarette. His thick black plastic glasses were held together by masking tape.

"A guy wrote a book about this place," he said.

I glanced at Lauren.

He pointed behind him to the apartment Masako and I had once lived in for five months. "He and his wife stayed there. It's in the book."

"Really?" I said.

"I kid you not," he said, lighting a Faro. He gestured across the darkened scene. "All this—the swimming pool, the restaurant, even the family that owns this place—it's in the guy's book."

"Interesting," Lauren said.

"Well, *buenas noches*."

When we'd walked back through the garden and were out of earshot, Lauren burst out laughing. "Why didn't you say something?"

"I was too surprised. Besides, he was dead drunk."

I told Lauren about the photographer who had approached me outside my house earlier in the evening.

"Maybe it's good you're doing some traveling," she said. "You're in a hall of mirrors here."

Outside the hotel the cobbled street was empty but for a lone taxi moving slowly past. I asked Lauren when she was leaving.

"The week after Christmas." She looked at me earnestly. "We'll stay in touch."

"Of course."

"And come see us when you're in New York."

"I will. My love to Celia. I'm sure she'll be okay."

It felt unreal, Lauren leaving. We threw our arms around each other in a long *abrazo*.

A chain of firecrackers erupted somewhere up on the mountain. We turned and looked up. A flower-spray of colored sparks burst in the sky. Then a *globo*, one of those multicolored, candle-lit paper balloons Mexicans love to loft toward the heavens, floated into view. It bisected the tip of the Parroquia, crossed the moon, then sank into the hillside somewhere.

"Such a fucking pretty town," Lauren said.

The next afternoon I went to the wedding of Juan José Sánchez, whom I still thought of as an ill-defined, gangly adolescent kid who liked to fix machines. But there he was at the altar of San Francisco Church, tall and proud and handsome in a fine dark suit, becoming a husband and father at nineteen. He'd hoped to be a *licenciado*, a lawyer—he certainly had the head and ambition for it—but now he needed money and was working as an ironmonger's assistant.

San Francisco Church, with its massive stone facade and formalistic interior, always struck me as chilly, devoid of feeling, lacking the Indian presence. Junípero Serra's missions in the Sierra Gorda had art and mystery, as did so many other churches and chapels in San Miguel: the Santa Ana, the Oratorio, San Juan de Dios, the little neighborhood chapels—and of course the grand Parroquia, with its nutty dripcastle facade. San Francisco, a block above the jardín, felt like a church where bureaucrats would go to worship, and they did. But the priest was popular, something of a draw. I'd attended a funeral oration there of a friend, a theater director, who'd faithfully attended every Sunday for years and swore by the priest.

Juan José's bride, Beatriz, looked ravishing—like a movie star, like Raquel Welch. It wasn't hard to see why Juan José had fallen. She wore a shimmering white silk dress that must have set her family back two years' salary. Throughout the ceremony, which lasted an hour and a half, Beatriz, her huge dark eyes downcast, held her bouquet demurely over her tummy. Lupe, Juan José's mother, had confided she was four months *embarazada*.

Juan José was Lupe's only son. His father had taken up with a woman in Texas and never come back. Today it was an uncle who stood in for him before the altar beside Lupe, a stout, bespectacled woman of deep faith and considerable intelligence who cooked and cleaned houses in the town and had raised Juan José, Juanita, and Alicia on sheer determination. Alicia was still only fourteen, and Juanita, the older one, had taken up with Chuy, the head of a local gang, to Lupe's great distress. Chuy, thick and pockmarked, with a greasy gang haircut and tattoos, sat hunkered in a rear pew, glowering; Juanita, much taller, sat beside him, looking sullen and disinterested. So Juan José was emerging as the pillar of the family. But how could either family pay for such a fancy wedding?

The ceremony was ornate, didactic, interminable. The

priest offered up homilies embedded within the matrix of church, God, and Jesus Christ—marriage as the unfolding of the divine plan. But how were Juan José and Beatriz going to make it on his wage? When the pressures grew too much, would Juan José follow the pattern of his father and defect? Near the end they knelt before the intoning priest, ribbons draped over their shoulders, their marriage now consummated in the eyes of the church, gorgeous Beatriz still heroically holding her wilting bouquet over her bulge.

Afterward guests, family, bride, and groom gathered outside in the courtyard beneath the stately trimmed laurels amid the vendors of *chicharrones* and *gelatinas*. Everyone seemed happy. I offered my *felicidades* to Juan José, Beatriz, and Lupe. They invited me, the lone gringo in attendance, to a reception and fiesta at a restaurant in town. I had to get home and pack; I was leaving early the next morning for Guanajuato, then to the States for Christmas. I looked for traces of relief in their eyes when I declined but saw only sincere disappointment.

Lupe listens to XESQ, Radio San Miguel, while she works, following closely the news of the community. She speaks with affection of *la gente*, the ordinary people among whom she lives. From La Luz, a growing community above town of modest brick houses partially subsidized by the government, she takes a bus to the center where she works in the big houses. She shops at the traveling Tuesday market and at Gigante, the new supermarket, both just a walk across the highway from her neighborhood. She has cable TV and a phone line in the house now; and Juan José has signed them up for Prodigy so they can be on the

Internet. In a way, Lupe lives a more modern life than those of us down in the old town in our big, unheated, eighteenth-century houses, shopping at the local markets, living among used things. Juan José and Beatriz will move in with her until the baby comes, or until they have enough money to move to their own place, which could be years from now.

9.

Fitzcarraldo and Dr. Leroy

In the fallow months of the year, passings are commemorated throughout Mexico. Guanajuato, city of masques and reveries, fictions and *fantasmas*—a place Edgar Allan Poe might have dreamed up—celebrates death all year long at the mummy museum, a short walk from the city center. Some find visiting these desiccated relics a ghoulish experience; others take them in with necrophilic glee. A mineral peculiarity of the soil in the cemetery nearby confers the dubious fate of physical immortality on local corpses whose descendants haven't kept up payment on grave plots. The ravaged specimen of Dr. Leroy from France, stiff dungarees forever sagging at his hips, oval mouth set in a permanent howl, never fails to leave me bemused. This frontier physician died in 1865, and with no one around to pay his fees, he was resurrected as a mummy in 1970. Does it console the good doctor somehow to know that his Chinese cook is there beside him, a mummy too?

The mummies, long a favorite Mexican postcard to send home, tease Mexico's rich relationship to the subject of death. This comfort with *la muerte*, the affection lavished on skeletons and skulls, the attitude of warm sentiment and humor, the blending of morbidity and wit, northerners often find alarming. If mummy-viewing is a chance to consider mortality in general, it is also an opportunity to note the peculiar persistence of certain body elements. That fingernails continue to grow after death is a well-known fact; but the endurance of public hair in skin shrunk over a century's time to the appearance of a saddle-bag comes as a surprise, unless you happen to be a gravedigger.

Once I visited the museum while it was in the process of overhaul, the mummies awaiting transfer to the newly built glass sarcophagi where they presently reside. Unwilling to lose revenue, they'd left the museum open, the mummies simply propped up against the walls, and I could reach out and touch the remains of Dr. Leroy. Stroking his crusty hip with my fingers, I remember thinking that we all are, in the end, leather.

Guanajuato, the first inland Mexican city I'd ever visited, held an enduring romance for me. Crumbling, operatic Guanajuato, with its heaped architecture and twisting medieval streets; its cool stone labyrinth of subterranean tunnels and great ruins from the silver mines that had endowed its patrons with centuries of wealth; its university, museums, churches, and government buildings of pink and green quarried stone. Guanajuato, with its bookshops and student cafés, serpentine lanes, worn tinted walls, and little *plazuelas.*

A mere hour away from San Miguel, it was utterly different: if San Miguel was *sol*, Guanajuato was *sombra.* People from San Miguel were always quick to praise Guanajuato but seldom visited except to attend the yearly Cervantino arts festival or on a day trip to show visiting guests. But I'd always suspected that had I not settled in San Miguel, I might have ended up here. Now with an empty house at my disposal for a few days before my flight to California from the airport nearby, I wanted to try the city on for size.

On a sharp and sunny pre-Christmas morning, I emerged from dark, dripping San Diego Tunnel running from Mellado, the neighborhood where I was staying, to the city center. (In Guanajuato people daily walk or drive through tunnels as if it were the most normal way to get around.) I emerged on Calle Positos, a few doors from the house where the artist Diego Rivera was born. A small museum now, it belatedly memorializes the massive painter, demoted in his lifetime to the status of a nonperson in Guanajuato for his sympathies with anticlericals during the Catholic counterrevolution of 1926–29, and for being a Marxist.

Guanajuato is a walker's city, with nary a straight street to be found, most of them impassable by car. One little lane off the Plaza San Fernando is so narrow a barrel-shaped indentation had to be hewn out of a wall to allow burros to pass; another allows lovers to kiss across balconies. Woven into a steep river valley, Guanajuato has all the packed interiority, the ruminative hallucination, of an Arab medina. A city where you are lost a priori is a city made for a man with a self-diagnosed case of dissociative fugue.

Turning up Positos, which changes its name several times in its brief, winding course past the towering university, I hopped on and off the narrow sidewalk, deferring to approaching walkers, they to me. In October, during the annual Cervantino Festival, these central streets become nearly impassable as revelers, tourists, concertgoers, musicians, mimes, and magicians fill the city. For three weeks the plazas, theaters, and churches ring day and night with music, dance, and drama from all over the world. Even in this pre-Christmas lull I passed a man carrying a tuba, a couple of Japanese Butoh dancers with white powdered faces, a street serenader still in ruffled collar and full Renaissance garb from the night before—and in the Plaza Baratillo, a skinny Santa Claus sipping hot *atole*, corn drink, from a paper cup. None of these apparitions raised much attention.

The little Baratillo's fluted fountain, a gift from the city of Florence during the fin de siècle reign of the dictator Porfirio Díaz, gathered around it flower, fruit, and vegetable vendors, an armada of pigeons, louche students lounging on green metal benches in the early sun, an Internet place, a café. Residents of Alameda and Mexiamora, the two neighborhoods up the winding hill behind, threaded their way among wandering tourists, Lonely Planets or Routards in hand. The Baratillo, crisscrossed by life, is a plaza of artists and mystics, rich in myth. People say that *fantasmas*, ghosts, hover here; that *la llorona*, Mexico's weeping woman, makes nightly visitations; that a *bruja*, a sorceress who once resided on Callejón Ave María, a tiny lane just above the flower sellers, still presides from her present station as a mummy in the museum.

Mornings in Guanajuato belong to the *caminantes*, the walkers. It wasn't hard for me to fall in love with a city where every few blocks a ceramic plaque commemorated a local writer dead and gone: *"Aqui vivía el genial cronista del pueblo . . ."* (Here lived the brilliant writer of the city . . .). Jorge Ibargüengoitia, a witty, revered contemporary author, described Guanajuato, where he was born, as "almost a phantom, a ghost."

In the covered Pasaje de los Arcos, off the grand Plaza Mayor, a simple blue and white plaque with the words *"La llegada de Alexander von Humboldt, 8 Agosto 1803"* commemorates the arrival on that day of the great German naturalist and explorer, a decidedly fugue-afflicted traveler, at the end of his epic three-year voyage through Latin America. Humboldt stayed at a house on this plaza that belonged to Colonel Diego Rul, one of the owners of the vastly rich Valenciana mine. Deeply impressed by Guanajuato, and having studied mining (along with philosophy, physics, languages, art, administration, botany, and astronomy), Humboldt lingered here among the great mines and the families that owned them before returning to Europe, where he spent the next twenty-seven years completing his thirty-volume work on his voyages, a sizable section devoted to his time in Guanajuato. (A lifelong liberal, adamantly opposed to slavery, Humboldt was a fast friend of Simón Bolívar, who said of him that he'd done more for the

Americas than all the conquistadors combined. At the age of sixty, Humboldt's unquenchable fugue—or perhaps better, in his case, wanderlust—drove him on a year's expedition across Russia to the desert wastes bordering China.)

Working my way upward along Calle Cantarranas, I peered down at the suddenly exposed Hidalgo Tunnel running beneath the city, the painted square facades of its ateliers clinging impossibly to the stone walls above. Built to channel the city's main riverbed, the tunnel was expanded, after a succession of floods in the nineteenth century, to allow more water to pass. To do this, the entire city floor and everything on it— streets, churches, convents, houses—was raised thirty feet. A glass display in the ground beside the Templo San Diego, across from the central Jardín de la Unión, revealed this miracle of retrofitting. An old convent lurked down there too beneath street level, sacrificed to the construction of the theater next door.

I took a seat on a bench in the Jardín de la Unión, opposite the small Greco-Roman Teatro Juárez. Men in worn suits sat beneath trimmed plane trees reading newspapers, having their shoes shined. Students and tourists clustered on the theater steps, taking in the winter sun. The dramatic *teatro*, with its wide steps, beefy columns, and statues of the six theatrical muses atop, stirred memories of my first arrival in Guanajuato.

"*Fitzcarraldo,*" I whispered aloud.

In Werner Herzog's film of that name, the German actor Klaus Kinski played a man fanatically obsessed with bringing an opera house up the Amazon River to the remote town of

Iquitos, convinced of the power of great European art to transform and enlighten, to tame the inscrutable dark—a bittersweet, ruinous conceit. Yet here was Fitzcarraldo's dream, alive in Guanajuato, in this little jeweled opera house begun during the reign of Porfirio Díaz: an oasis of splendor in the far provinces.

The Teatro Juárez had hosted the great international opera stars of its day; then after the revolution it fell upon hard times, even becoming a movie house for a while after World War II. In 1972 the Cervantino Festival—which takes as its theme Cervantes's Don Quixote, a fitting symbol for this city of phantasms and toppling fancies—brought it back to life as a theater. On different occasions since, I'd heard New York's Kronos Quartet play Thelonious Monk here, the university's symphony orchestra tackle Shostakovich. And whenever I visited the city and came upon one of the many wrought-iron statues of the festival's patron, Don Quixote, atop his rickety steed, I saw not just that dreamer of La Mancha but the actor Klaus Kinski—maniacal blue bug eyes, scrambled blond mop, crooked quivering lips—as Fitzcarraldo/Quixote.

Behind the Teatro Juárez, a steep hillside, stacked with multihued houses, rose to a massive pink stone statue of a man holding a torch. This great-thighed fire-bringer—who resembles some combination of Prometheus, a Marvel Comics hero, Joseph Stalin, and the Michelin Man—commemorates a local liberator, nicknamed Pipila, who set fire to the Alhondiga granary gates on September 28, 1810, allowing Hidalgo's troops to win the first battle of the independence movement against

Spain. For a few heady weeks Guanajuato became the rebel capital, until Hidalgo was captured and shot in Chihuahua, his head sent here to be exhibited in a cage hung from a pike on the granary wall for ten years—alongside Pipila's, and San Miguel's insurgent Colonel Ignacio Allende's—as a lesson to the insurgent populace. But Pipila's words, "There are still other Alhondigas to burn," ignited further revolts that prevailed, immortalizing these three, their names emblazoned upon buildings, towns, streets, and shops across Mexico.

An oxygen-robbing ascent up a web of coiled *callejones* brought me to Pipila's huge pink feet and a dizzying vista of the maze I'd just emerged from. Everything interior now lay spread below, a breathing map—the teatro, the jardín, plazas and streets and lanes, all crammed into dynamic proximity. I could see, jutting above the rooflines, domes and spires, churches and cathedrals, the university facade, the huge Alhondiga granary, and the Hidalgo market clocktower, designed by Paris's Alexandre Eiffel. Houses painted in uncountable pastel tints crowded the surrounding mountains. Visitors often try to describe Guanajuato in terms of other places—Lisbon, Toledo, Valparaíso, Urbino, Tangier—before surrendering to its utter singularity.

A rhythmic, repetitive sound drifted up from below, separating out from traffic noise. I could just make out a collection of moving figures in the Plaza de la Paz, across from the grand old government buildings. The sounds congealed into human chanting—a celebration or demonstration or rally of some sort. No day in Mexico goes uncommemorated—a favored saint, a patriotic occasion, just about anything warrants a fiesta or procession. Here in the state capital groups regularly brought complaints, demands, or enthusiasms before the government.

Descending by way of another route, I came back out onto Calle Juárez, farther along. From there I let gravity guide me down, veering off into the quiet little squares, the *plazuelas*. San Fernando, perhaps my favorite, offered views of the surrounding polychromed houses and shops from its outdoor cafés, restaurants, and bookstalls. A connecting path led to little Plaza San Roque, where the Cervantino began in 1972; now it was a permanent nightly performance space with a few outdoor bleachers across from its old church. From there stairs wound down to the statelier Plazuela La Reforma, with its trees and benches and fountain, feeding me back out onto Calle Juárez.

The Mercado Hidalgo, a soaring metal shell of a building big enough to house a couple of dirigibles, was another extravagance of the Díaz era. It was originally intended as a train station, but with the decline of the railways it became instead the city's grand market. I didn't enter so much as penetrate the Mercado Hidalgo—for an entire parallel, exterior *mercado* gathered around its fringes: flower and blanket and bread sellers, food stalls serving *menudo* and *pozole*, sellers of cassettes and tortillas and matches and curative herbs. *"¡Escojale!"* cried the vendors. (Choose one!) *"¡Barato!"* (Cheap!) I edged my way among symmetrically piled displays of foods whose very names were colors: orange, lime, melon, papaya, avocado. Village women in aprons and braids sat cross-legged on colorful oilcloth before fresh blue-corn tortillas, shaved *nopales* (cactus), cheeses, and *salsas picantes*.

An American supermarket is a depopulated assembly of shelves; a Mexican market is spectacle. A visit to an American supermarket is dispatched with—items checked off against a list, merchandise packed into the car, a solitary car ride home. A visit to *el mercado* might provide an entire morning's entertainment, requiring as much time to tell about as to visit. The abundant Aztec marketplaces the first Spaniards described were not so different from today's great emporia in Guadalajara and Mexico City, or the sprawling provincial markets, or the village open-air stalls with items spread on blankets in the bright sun. Not merely foods of all kinds but almost anything else one might desire can be found in *el mercado*: clothes, baskets, furniture, household items, music, curative herbs, charms. The Mexican market is total immersion. *"¡Escojale!"* How could anyone be depressed at a Mexican market?

Once inside the great building, I elbowed my way past dry goods and food stalls to a stool at Lonchería El Chino where, ravenous from my walk, I ordered a *torta de pierna* (pork leg sandwich) and a banana and strawberry *licuado*. Sipping my drink, I looked around at the *carnitas* and *mariscos* stands, the sellers of brooms and baskets and folk arts. Activity along the floor was muted by the sheer height, the boomy vastness, of the art nouveau building. Light entered through tall arched windows along either end. High along the walls, an open second level housed more stalls.

The market, though busy enough, seemed less crowded

than I remembered from earlier visits. A few stalls were boarded up; others displayed fewer goods. A big modern supermarket had opened down the street where the old bus station had once been; I wondered if it was drawing people off. New department and discount stores had sprung up in the centro as well. Would the great Mexican mercados, whose origins far predated the Spanish invasion, survive? I didn't want to think that this extravagant old structure would one day be converted into a lifeless mall.

Wide strutwork metal stairs led to the market's second level, where I wandered into a deserted administrative office hung with old sepia photos of the city during the time of the building's construction. City of *piedra*, stone, beautiful even then, raised from hard earth by the hands of poor workers. The Mercado Hidalgo, with its Parisian clocktower, had bestowed a temporal vision of beauty no less ephemeral, it now seemed, than the silver wealth that had made it possible. Like the mines in the hills surrounding it, like the rubber boom in Fitzcarraldo's Brazil, tides of wealth swept in, swept out.

At its early peak, ninety thousand lived and worked in Guanajuato, though that number dwindled to eight thousand after the 1910 Revolution. As recently as the 1960s one writer commented on the listlessness and defeat that had settled over the city and wondered why people even stayed. Now the town had risen anew as a business, agriculture, and mining center, close enough to the border to draw some U.S. industry yet far enough away to avoid its *maquiladora* oppressions. As if to embody its resurrection from the near-dead, Guanajuato resident and former governor Vicente Fox, a tall, mustachioed rancher and former Coca-Cola executive, was now the country's president.

Still, Guanajuato was inexorably falling apart, for even stone yields to time's attrition. This was part of its rich romantic appeal, of course: the slumping infrastructure, the sagging dwellings clinging to their hillsides, the old dry goods stores and fabric shops rooted in the 1950s that allowed reverie and imagination to circulate.

Back on the streets, traffic had slowed as siesta time neared. At the Plaza de la Paz the demonstration I'd heard from the mountain was dispersing. A few student protesters had left behind on a government building wall an amazingly well-drawn graffito: George Bush as the mummy Dr. Leroy, his face contorted in the rictus of a scream—and beside him, Mexican *presidente* Vicente Fox as his mummified Chinese cook.

Mellado, an old mining district on the mountain east of the city center, was the birthplace of the rebel hero Pipila, in the days when its great Rayas silver mine had rained wealth, if upon too few. In the canyon beneath the mine's looming stone bulwarks, the vast ex-hacienda Duran had long ago been dismantled, subdivided into a populous neighborhood of workers and artisans now known as Barrio Nuevo, where I was staying.

Climbing the steep hill back to the house late that afternoon, I passed a wiry old man steering a wheelbarrow loaded with bricks, the same man I'd passed when I left in the morning.

He did this all day on little more than refrescos from the tienda. No wonder the young men headed to the States to find work.

Realizing I'd had nothing to eat or drink, I began looking for a *tiendita*, a little neighborhood store. Even the poorest Mexican neighborhood has one, usually announced by a Coca-Cola or Fanta sign, or a bare lightbulb hanging outside. A typical tiendita is a nutritionist's nightmare: cheap candy bars, soft drinks, white bread. Yet if you ask, they may also have fresh eggs from a cousin's ranch, or tortillas or *bolillos*, the Mexican staple bread roll, delivered daily. Some carry vegetables and fruits, and these days most have refrigeration.

Ducking to enter a tiny, unlit tiendita near the house where I was staying, I stood on a dirt floor with barely enough space to move. Behind a curtain a baby gurgled, and a *telenovela* flickered on the TV. I noticed on the shelves Instant Cup O'Soup, Colgate, Camay, and Snickers among the Mexican brand names.

"*Buenas tardes,*" I called.

A señora appeared from behind the curtain, wiping her hands on her apron. "*Sí, señor. ¿Qué le doy?*"

I bought a large bottle of orange Fanta, a few bolillos. Envisioning eggs for dinner, I also bought a packet of processed Kraft cheese, fresh eggs, *calabaza* squash, an onion, tomatoes, and tortillas. She rummaged in her apron and, coin by coin, extracted change.

"*Gracias.*"

"*Al contrario. Que le vaya bien.*"

As far from a 7-Eleven as you could get. The experience

had been warm, direct, and polite, delivered with an Indian-Spanish-Mexican grace that seemed instinctive. Back outside, I straightened up and gingerly bore my clear plastic bag full of eggs and the other groceries up the precipitous, stony road to the house, accompanied by a few neighborhood mutts.

Outside my door I fell into conversation with a couple of neighbors, guys who worked across the border, leaving pieces of lives somewhere in Texas, California, Chicago—in Los Estados, as they called it. They'd come back home for Christmas fiestas and winter harvest. Talking to me affirmed a connection, as talking to Mexicans sometimes did for me in California. Both men worked on construction crews—one in Houston, one in Atlanta. They crossed twice a year, paying a coyote, as the runners are called, close to $3,000 for the illegal voyage by truck direct from Guanajuato, payoffs prearranged along the way on both sides. Most trips succeeded, though sometimes things went badly; then there were wanderings in the desert, violence, hunger, arrests—and for some, death far from home. Recounting a couple of bad crossings, they laughed bitterly. *Nunca se sabe,* they said. You never know. They'd return again in February, after the rainy season, when the big construction projects renewed up north. I'd make my crossing by plane in a couple of days, in relative comfort, paying far less, and I'd return sooner too—*ojalá,* God willing.

The house, which belonged to friends of friends, sat on a hillside just below the Panorámica, the scenic road circling the city. It had heavy wooden furniture, terra-cotta tile floors, blue and white ceramic dishware from nearby Dolores Hidalgo, and a hand-carved wooden statue of Saint Francis of Assisi in the corner of the *sala*. Plate-glass windows offered a wide view of Cerro del Cuarto, the barrio directly across the steep canyon.

From the downstairs living room, I watched the sun drop into the mountain cleft. The piled cubist arrangement of buildings opposite flared red. All that earth and stone and brick and rebar and plaster, coaxed up into dwellings on these precarious hillsides. Trees along these once-forested mountains were sparse now, centuries of wood sacrificed to the mines, the construction of homes, or firewood on cold winter nights like this one promised to be. The houses high up were painted, those below not, rough signifiers of wealth. But as in other areas of Mexican life, what appeared to be shabbiness bore, upon closer inspection, an order dictated by circumstance. Building surfaces were often kept rough, rebars exposed, as an unfinished house incurred a lower tax burden.

As twilight deepened, the buildings became simply shapes, their details lost. They began to resemble the old Indian dwellings hewn into mountain clefts in New Mexico and northern Arizona—Canyon de Chelly, the Anasazi ruins.

With nightfall, lights bloomed across the canyon, revealing an animated wonderland of Christmas displays. A decade ago that hill would have been almost dark—one measure of progress, I supposed. Dogs' howls arose in chorus from somewhere in the canyon. A bell pealed at the old Mellado Church at the top of the hill, above the Rayas mine, tolling the hour of seven. Feeling cold from the floor tiles through my shoes, I decided to make a fire upstairs in the bedroom, though I didn't relish the thought of digging through the woodpile out back where scorpions lurked.

Then as I stood up, I heard children's voices outside.

In the dark, stony street, a cluster of kids stood before a neighbor's house, holding lit candles and singing. These were the twelve nights of *posadas*, when children, enacting the search for the holy manger, go from house to house asking for lodging, only to be turned away by all but the designated family—my neighbor this Christmas, apparently, as the door swung open to a simple dwelling, and the singing children, bearing their candles, filed in out of the cold.

If you want to have culture, a Brazilian rubber baron counseled the hapless Fitzcarraldo, laboring to float his opera house up the Amazon, first you must become rich. Guanajuato, founded in 1559, achieved that state overnight when silver was discovered. By the time of Humboldt's visit in 1803, silver had turned a local miner, Obregón, and a merchant, Otero, into the richest men in the world. A single mine, La Valenciana, is said to have produced a fifth of the silver circulating in the world until 1910. Though La Valenciana still functioned, I felt more poignancy than awe the next morning picking silver-specked shards from the mounds of slate-colored tailings, peering fifteen hundred feet down the vertiginous shaft, gazing up at the once-busy pyramidal *hornos*, the ovens.

San Caetano Church, where Valenciana's vice-regal crowd once came to pray, towered dramatically on a plummeting hillside above the town—a hymn to rococo excess. Its high, peeling walls echoed the footsteps of tourists and the chirpings of small black birds wheeling in the cathedral's towering cupola. What did they subsist on, the birds, I wondered: the peeling gold leaf of the immense altars stained white with their droppings? Outside, vendors hawked geodes from the mines.

Back at the house, I made a lunch of leftovers and packed for my flight to California that evening. Then I took a fifteen-minute climb up to the Rayas mine, whose huge bulwarks I'd seen from the house. Leaning over a circular stone wall, I gazed down through a dark assemblage of old cables into the mine's indiscernible bowels, where a team of young engineers was laboring to make Rayas productive again—I could hear the lumbering whine of its old winches—but barely breaking even, I was told. Only four of Guanajuato's original thirty-four mines now remained open, the rest brought down by revolution, mercury poisoning, and the collapse of world silver prices.

It was a bright winter day a mile up in the Mexican highlands. From a parapet jutting out over the valley of Guanajuato, I watched clouds speed over mountaintops marked by bare crosses, the statue of Pipila just visible above central Guanajuato's ravine. Local kids clustered around, offering tours of the mine or simply begging pesos for a *"chesco,"* a soft drink. Inside the rampart walls I came upon a little sunken stone amphitheater, clotted with weeds, where the mine owners and their families had once staged little productions, or held forth to their staff.

A further climb brought me to the half-ruined church of Mellado, whose bells I'd heard tolling from the house. A wizened docent showed me their prize possession—a dim, peeling mural of the Last Supper the church hoped to restore through donations.

I descended the winding panoramic road to the Cata mine, which was still producing enough gold and silver to support its miners' co-op. A little tree-shaded plaza had been built in honor of the apparition here of a renowned saint, El Señor de Villaseca. A little chapel surfaced with stone shards from the mines was crammed with snapshots, charms, letters of thanks—and the discarded poultices and crutches of children and loved ones healed by the saint's intercession.

My last stop before the airport was the small community of Marfil, at the foot of the city. Once home to Guanajuato's rich and mighty, it had hosted a small international colony of painters, homosexuals, and blacklisted screenwriters in the 1950s and 1960s. I knew some of them, or their children, or their ex-lovers, and had heard the stories of that brief sybaritic era. Climbing among Marfil's churches, broken aqueducts and ex-haciendas late that day put contemporary notions of wealth in perspective: the Hacienda San Gabriel de Barrera, with its grand stone house, private chapel, and myriad gardens, once required a staff of three thousand servants. It was administered by the government these days, for what family could possibly afford to buy such a place, let alone keep it up?

As the taxi approached the little Bajio airport at dusk, I saw the Aeromexico jet poised on the runway, and I didn't want to leave. I wanted to be back with Fitzcarraldo, Quixote, and Dr. Leroy, rummaging among the dross of dreams.

10.

La Frontera

The Aeromexico vaulted over the dry northern states, then westward toward the darkening horizon line of the Pacific. I sat at a window seat, thinking about the magazine editor's brief, the feature article I'd been commissioned to write by spring. What was new and interesting in Mexico these days? Immersed in my voyages, I sometimes forgot to see things in those terms. Border to border, coast to coast, Mexico offered a boundless *canasta* of riches; yet I experienced these journeys less as a catalog of attractions than as a succession of illuminations, discoveries, and encounters with a necessary Other—myself, of course, in new guises, revealed in reflection off the alien surfaces travel provides. Other times I felt I was sifting among ruins and resurrections, mining for intimations of a new order lurking in the husk of the old—a pathway out of a terminal impasse as our world, once again, cracked at its seams.

The plane was filled with Mexicans returning to work in

the States or to visit relatives for Christmas. Somewhere below us stretched the vast, porous *frontera*, with its yawning expanses of desert, prairie, and mountains. Geography *is* fate, I thought. Imagine England and all of North Africa—Morocco, Algeria, Tunisia, Libya, Egypt—sharing a common, unguardable border. Across this mythical demarcation running from Tijuana/ San Diego all the way to Matamoros/Brownsville on the Caribbean, two deeply different societies gaze at each other, imagine each other, imitate each other, visit each other, resent each other, violate each other, and penetrate each other in every way imaginable. Labor and drugs and music and food flow north; money and hip-hop and merchandise and retirees flow south.

Vecinos distantes, distant neighbors for sure, my fellow passengers and I—yet in other unacknowledged ways as intimate as lovers, tangled in fitful clandestine embrace. Identities tug at each other across this trackless boundary we crossed. Words in Spanish drop their English italics: *tacos* became just tacos, as once in cowboy days *la riata* became lariat. Mexicans say "*adiós*, bye" and "*sí*, okay" and "website." U.S. presidential candidates parade their Latino credentials, angle for photo-ops wearing sombreros and munching burritos, while in Mexican cities Costco and Wal-Mart establish beachheads.

This great *intercambio*, involving countless millions of people and billions of dollars, often illicit, also showers hard-won blessings: a man who gets paid three dollars a day back home can make twelve an hour *en el otro lado* and wire a good portion of it home by Western Union—and in one of Mexico's countless poor, stacked *colonias* of unsurfaced brick and cement, electricity blooms, food appears on family tables, new school or football uniforms are purchased, and a student enters the university on the hill.

Living in the crosshairs of this cultural shift, I am both expression and instrument of it: double resident, hence double agent, in the service of both sides and neither. Spiritual migrant, permanent gringo, riding the tidal currents that surge across this semipermeable membrane, *la frontera.*

The lights of San Diego slid past below. I sat with a volume of Herman Melville's short stories that I'd come upon in a Guanajuato bookstall, probably left behind by some gringo. American writers, I thought, had always been beset by a kind of collective dissociative fugue—"sudden, unexpected wanderings from home." Melville, Edith Wharton, Henry James, Ezra Pound, Gertrude Stein, Ernest Hemingway, James Baldwin, Paul Bowles—full- or part-time wanderers or expatriates all. For these writers, being outside often provided the best seat in the house: neither quite here nor there, yet in both places at once. "The act of comparison," wrote the American writer Donald Richie, a longtime resident of Japan, "is the act of creation."

Now America was instinctively drawing up its moats. Travel would change, both its nature and its meaning. The world beyond our borders would be viewed with greater suspicion and fear. More now than ever, we'd need these voices at a distance, exemplars of an essential American breed, calling back to us from across *la frontera*, reminding us to widen our gaze.

At LAX, a greeting of armed soldiers and sniffing dogs. On the freeways, in front of homes, flying flags. I'd returned to a country under siege: the disturbance, the fear was palpable. On "news" stations, war drums were beating, new enemies identified. A professor friend with a draft-age son, beside herself with worry about the possible reinstitution of the draft, said, "Tell me about Mexico. Should we start learning Spanish, consider emigrating there?"

Still the danger, for all but a few, remained abstract—dread of harm from an unseen direction. The daily enemy, it was becoming clear, was the fear itself. The small courage of continuing to do what one did taught resilience. The holiday season gave license to hope. Arise and act. My friend David Lebrun continued preparations to shoot his film on Mayan writing in Guatemala, Honduras, and southern Mexico; I planned to meet up with him and his crew at Palenque in early February. The night before leaving for San Francisco to join Masako and her family for Christmas, I heard Lila Downs sing in Spanish, English, and Mixtec to a packed audience in an L.A. club, and the *frontera*, all *fronteras*, seemed very thin.

On a clear, chilly morning I set out up Highway 101 north, the old El Camino Real that Junípero Serra had forged, mission by mission—Santa Barbara, San Luis Obispo, San Miguel, nineteen in all. Passing through towns and fields worked for generations by Mexicans, I saw Serra's epic passage across California now in the light of those five fanciful, art-rich little prototypes I'd visited a few months earlier in the Sierra Gorda.

Reaching Salinas early that afternoon, I turned west and drove toward the sea. Beneath a windswept bluff of cypresses and sand, I stood in the adobe compound of Carmel Mission, gazing into a simple monk's cell, nearly identical to the one in the Sierra Gorda, where Serra—another sort of Quixote indeed—had ended his earthly mission.

By the time Serra and his friars reached Carmel, their future headquarters, the ships that were to have met them there with guns and supplies, thinking them lost or killed, had gone on, leaving behind only a wooden cross on a hill overlooking the bay as a sign. Meanwhile, Indians from the Carmel River Valley had hung fish, dead animals, and flayed skins from the cross, smeared dried blood on it, carved symbols into it, paganized it. To little avail, in the end: of all the tribes the Franciscans had come to liberate from heathen darkness, none would survive into this century. But the Carmel Indians' gesture resonates in the mind.

On a biting, windswept Christmas afternoon, Masako and I took a walk at Land's End, San Francisco's farthest promontory. From a wooded bluff above the sea we looked back at the Golden Gate Bridge, draped like a pendant across the bay, streaming with cars. A young couple passed us pushing a stroller with triplets. From a car radio somewhere, Charles Brown's "Merry Christmas Baby" segued into José Feliciano's

"Feliz Navidad," a Mexican favorite. A freighter passed beneath the bridge on its way to dock, another outbound to a distant port.

Soon we'd begin another year back in Mexico—she to Oaxaca to work on her exhibitions, me to further journeys, eager to inscribe more onto the Mexican postcard I'm always writing home.

Two

"I don't believe it's true what they say, that as you travel you
become a different person. What happens is that you grow
lighter, you shed your obligations and your past just as you
reduce everything you possess to the few items you need
for your luggage."

—ANTONIO MUÑOZ MOLINA, *SEPHARAD*

11.

The Yellow House

City of coffee and orchids, the guidebooks like to say. Clambering stiffly off the bus, I thought for a moment I really did smell those orchids.

As there'd been no arrangement, I didn't expect anybody to meet me. I had only one name here, a friend of a friend in Mexico City, an architect named Servin. Still, I half-expected somebody to be standing there in the foggy evening. But there was only a small man with cropped hair in a blue uniform collecting my luggage from beneath the bus and beckoning me to follow him to a taxi.

As the little Toyota wended into the city, I tried to read shapes through the mist. Clumps of trees fell off below to my left, lights of hillocks beyond. To my right, buildings crowded down to the street, ample old colonials and contemporary hodge-podge. The hazy hills and drizzle reminded me somehow of central Japan. I knew that Xalapa, situated in the cool mountains above Veracruz, lay along an old trade route to Mexico City and that it was the provincial capital where the wealthy from the sweltering, insect-plagued Caribbean coast had once stored their families and their holdings.

"Our famous *chipichipi*," the driver said, gesturing through the windshield. "It refreshes our City of Flowers every evening." He laughed. "It drives some people a little nuts. But I tell you this, señor. Here in Xalapa you will feel safe."

I knew little of the region, with its Olmec ruins and thrumming *son jarocho* music, though it did bear an appeal both anthropological and romantic. A half-recollected carnival weekend in the city of Veracruz years ago—marimbas, *mojitos*, *danzón*—surfaced, its details lost.

Traffic slowed along an artery called Xalapeños Ilustres, a name so florid I almost expected the road to be lined with busts and statues. It seemed to be Jalapa with either a J or an X, as written on the front of the bus I'd taken from Mexico City to get here. The word itself, I'd read in a guidebook, was a Spanish brutalization of the Nahuatl term meaning "springs of sandy water."

Lonely Planet described the Hotel Limón, with tiled walls and pleasant interior courtyard, as "an excellent bargain choice," but my journalist friend Eduardo in Mexico City had mentioned another called the Hotel California. The idea of staying in a place enshrining a homegrown pop epic was too toothsome to pass up.

The taxi wheeled right at the corner of Primo Verdad—with street names like these, Xalapa was already getting on my good side—circled a tiny unlit plaza, and came to a halt. The hotel's sign was unlit and unreadable in the dark, though as I passed beneath it I could just make out that it really did say HOTEL CALIFORNIA.

They sold soft drinks, shampoo, and condoms downstairs at the desk. At first I thought it might be a whorehouse. Was this a joke of Eduardo's? But the second-floor room was high, white, and silent, with pale green tile floors, a tall oval mirror, and a bare hanging bulb. A rattan chair, a wooden clothing rack, and two double beds completed the furnishings. Green wooden shutters opened onto a tiny balcony above the little plaza. I threw my bags onto one bed and lay down on the other, still in my clothes.

It had been a long day's journey. An Aeromexico red-eye from L.A. had landed me in Mexico City just past dawn. For the length of a rattling morning ride across the clotted, smog-stung capital, I'd listened to a taxi driver rail against that *cabrón* Presidente Fox, ex-governor of my state of Guanajuato. Then the hot, turning bus trip eastward through glaring sun and pale empty mountains, past gypsum digs and cactus farms, ever deeper into eastern Mexico, while Schwarzenegger blew away the world on the video monitors at max volume and the wide blue Mexican afternoon condensed into inscrutable fog.

I must have dozed off on the hotel bed, for when I awoke light was pooling onto the tile floor through an open shutter. A church's low soothing bell marked a time not coincident with the digital travel clock I'd placed on the bed table. I sat up, startled by the sudden feeling that somebody was asleep in the other bed, but it was just my own luggage piled there.

I walked to the wrought-iron balcony. Though it was just past ten, silence blanketed the deserted plaza. Distant heavy metal thumped from some club or bar. A half-dozen crows wheeled out of the mist and swooped past, cawing. The aroma of burnt maize reached me. I could just make out the straw sombrero in the plaza below, a lone seller with his metal bucket full of roasted corn.

Suddenly Mexico flooded in, erupted behind my eyes, in my chest. *¡México querido y lindo!* Turning back to the room, I felt a wild, fugitive happiness I associated with earlier days in this soulful, benighted country, intimations of a life lived closer to the bone. Here in Xalapa you can feel safe, the taxi driver had said. I wanted to believe that, that I'd found a seam in the fraught world, respite from travels taken and those that lay ahead—a not unrestful place.

I took from my shoulder bag a book by another wanderer, Elizabeth Bishop. As I opened it, my eyes fell upon lines from her poem "Santarém."

> *I really wanted to go no farther;*
> *more than anything else I wanted to*
> *stay awhile.*

I awoke to soft, persistent knocking. My eyes opened upon a bright trapezoid of light on the green tiles.

"*¿Quién es?*"

"*Le espera un señor,*" a woman's voice answered.

I washed quickly at the cold-water tap and descended the wooden stairs to the lobby. A tall, large-jawed young man in a windbreaker and sneakers stepped forward and offered his hand.

"Gustavo Servin."

"Eduardo's friend."

"*Bienvenido a Xalapa.*"

The handshake collapsed into a Mexican abrazo—quick bear hug, paired back claps—an intimacy usually reserved for amigos, or a way of saying he was willing to be one.

We walked outside into the little plaza. Just then a wash of warm sunlight and color flooded us, diffusing the morning fog, recasting the plaza in subtropical hues. It was as if the muggy coast had risen to conquer the mountain mist. I'd never seen a faster, more dramatic weather change—from cool and drizzly to warm and tropical, black and white to Technicolor in a single dissolve.

"We live here in the mist, the *llovizna*, you see," Servin said. "But when it clears, it is something, no?"

Yes, it was. I followed Servin up Primo Verdad in the spreading glow, the air thick with the aroma of fresh coffee. We passed four cafés in the first block.

"From the local *cafeteros*, the coffee plantations," Servin said. "There are more cafés in Xalapa than you can count. I'll take you to one of my favorites."

We walked along sloping cobbled streets once built for

horses, past restaurants and tailor shops and chocolate stores, amid the colliding airs. Xalapa seemed to be a city of closures, then sudden openings to green mountains above and valleys below. I could still read, between belching buses and morning traffic, its colonial undercoat in the Baroque government buildings and patio-courtyards. Servin guided me across verdant plazas, through moist parks of orchid, hibiscus, and giant aurucaria, beside a lake where palms and pines grew beside each other on its banks. A silvery light, neither sun nor shade, settled around us, diffusing objects. And everywhere, the smell of fresh coffee.

"*Xalapa de la feria*, they called it," Servin said. "This is where the great fairs used to be held in colonial times."

From a parapet in the city's central plaza, I could see that we were at the foot of the mountain the bus had descended last night in fog. Its snowy peak floated above us in a ring of clouds. Servin gestured across the valley to a sprawl of buildings and stadiums on a bluff opposite. "The University of Veracruz. Sixty thousand students. I teach there."

I followed him down wide stairs and along another slanting street. We entered a café with the words LA PARROQUIA etched on its windows. Inside, white-jacketed waiters drizzled black coffee and hot milk into glasses from tin pots, proffered trays of Mexican pastries and breads amid a lively racket of conversations and clattering dishes.

Sipping my steaming *lechera*, I saw, two tables away, a man hunched over a book, nursing a coffee, an unfiltered cigarette burning down in an ashtray as he lit another. Strange and surprisingly pleasant, the smell of tobacco, the bookish scene. We could have been in Cambridge, Berkeley, a café in Madrid—only the coffee was fresher and better. A literary town! I'd reached the birthplace of Carlos Fuentes.

Servin brushed sugar crumbs off his chin with his napkin, then reached for another pastry. Outside, fog had moved back in, erasing sun and color as quickly as it had revealed it. "Welcome to *la zona de la niebla*," he said, calling for two more lecheras.

The zone of mists. Hardly what people imagine when they think of Mexico. It seemed almost perverse, living in "sunny Mexico" in this way. Yet the cool drizzle lent Xalapa a dreaminess, softening hard edges, inviting contemplation. My temples pulsed from the dense, steam-infused coffee.

"Think of Xalapa as Mexico's San Francisco. Or Seattle," Servin said. "Coffee, rain, the life of the mind. Poets love it, and musicians—we have our own symphony orchestra—and crazy architects like me. But when the sun comes out, it's a hot, tropical sun. And then if you like, an hour down the road you are swimming in the Caribbean." Servin took out a pack of Marlboro Lights. "So will you be in Xalapa awhile?"

"I'm planning some trips in the region. Veracruz, of course. Up the coast to Papantla. El Tajin, to see the ruins. The *son jarocho* festival in Tlacotalpan."

"Yes, you must go. And then?"

"The Yucatán. Possibly Chiapas. Then a trip to South America, I hope. Though with recent events, who knows?"

"Do wars ever end? Or is it always the same war?" Servin

tapped a cigarette from the pack and lit it. "But . . . listen, I have a little house to rent. If you'd be interested."

"Thanks, I don't think so. I'll be traveling about, and—"

"It might be cheaper for you. You need a base somewhere, no? Why not Xalapa? How much is the room at the Hotel California?"

"Eleven dollars a night." Hardly a back-breaking figure, even in Mexican terms.

"I can offer you my casita for two hundred dollars a month. You'd have more room. A kitchen, privacy. Shall we take a look? It's right around the corner."

Halfway down a plummeting street called Sebastián Camacho, Servin opened the padlock on a tall white metal gate. We climbed brick stairs slippery with green mold from Xalapa's unremitting damp, passing a low empty structure on our right. At the top we came to a small ruined garden, an old metal table and chairs sitting lopsided among creepers and wild orchids. Morning glories twined up the remains of a broken wall dense with patches of flaking pigment. Beside the garden stood a little ocher-toned casita.

Inside it was small, clean, and freshly painted white above and deep yellow below at the *faldón*, the waist-high dividing line. There was a wide mattress with bedding on the floor, a simple bare desk and chair, a gooseneck lamp. The kitchen had a cold-water sink, tile counter, minifridge, and hotplate, and in the bathroom a rudimentary shower, toilet, and covered bucket, as Mexicans don't flush their tissues. A window in the front room framed a perfect view over Xalapa's rooftops of Citlaltépetl, the snow-capped mountain we'd seen from the plaza.

It was sweet, monastic—beautiful.

"You can take it for a month. If you like it, then we'll see, no?"

Back at the corner of Xalapeños Ilustres and Primo Verdad, the sun reappeared, throwing up a rainbow directly in front of us, tilting the landscape and mood of the city yet again.

"So where will you go today?" Servin asked.

"Explore the city a little. The anthropology museum, for sure."

"Yes, you must see the Olmec heads."

We arrived at the little plaza in front of the Hotel California, with its whitewashed facade, red trim, and black balconies. Servin handed me his card. "Give me a call later. Tell me what you decide."

"Thanks, Gustavo. Honestly, I doubt I'll take it."

"*Sí, pero* . . ." He spread his hands and wriggled them in the Mexican gesture of equivocation.

"What?"

"The Hotel California. You know what they say. You can check out, but you can never leave."

I laughed at his command of the reference. Impossible to visit any country without hearing that song, it seemed. "Wherever you go," I said, "there's the Eagles. Why?"

"It's a mystery," Servin said, clapping me on the shoulder. "*Hasta pronto*, eh?"

They always looked so forbidding in photos, those massive Olmec heads—impassive, unpitying, staring straight on at you. Everybody's seen them in reproduction on the covers of tourist books or museum catalogs. Face to face with them, here in Xalapa's modern, plant-thronged Museo de Antropología, they seemed absolutely huge, more than twice my size in height, as wide and thick as they are high. How did the Olmecs get these stone colossi up the mountains from southern Veracruz a thousand years before Christ?

But seeing them up close from the side and back, not just the frontal view on the book covers, these pitted basalt giants, with their squashed wide faces, flat noses, and thick fluted lips, looked almost benign, friendly even—smiling slightly, sagely. Pre-Colombian peoples, usually portrayed as deadpan, must have laughed a lot if these heads, and the thousands of little grinning pinch-pottery figurines in the museum's Huastecan collection, are any indication. But they did look so *African*, the big ones. I could see how a heretical German-Mexican anthropologist, Alexander von Wuthenau, used them as evidence pointing to migrations from West Africa to the Veracruz coast long before the Spaniards came, suggesting African traces in the coastal population predating slavery.

Mexico's layered, ornate history, still only partially decoded, sometimes seemed such rich terra incognita to me, coming as I do from the land to the north, where history and memory are deleted daily; and living here seemed less an odyssey in an exotic foreign land than simply a chance to fill out the rest of my American self.

I spent midday exploring Xalapa's tangled central streets and lanes, ducking into quirky museums and bustling markets, pausing for another lechera in another café. Walking the serene lake paths below the hilly green campus of Veracruz University, I knew I was already falling in love a little with Xalapa.

At some point I realized I hadn't seen a single tourist. In one of the half-dozen bookstores along Xalapeños Ilustres, I asked for a Xalapa guidebook and was told none exists. "Cool, clean and civilized" was *Lonely Planet*'s brief verdict on the city. Six hours by car or bus from Mexico City, with no real airport, far more cafés than cantinas, and weather like this, Xalapa was hardly the place to work on your tan. Even the spelling of the city's name was unsettled, with its optional X or J.

As if to bring home the point, I went to a modern building across from the Parque Juárez in search of the tourist office. I found it upstairs, at the end of a dim corridor, a bucket and mop leaning up against a locked door with a frosted-glass pane that said in fading letters OFICINA DE TURISMO.

On Calle Diamante, one of Xalapa's little pedestrian streets, I had lunch at a restaurant called La Sopa and thought again about the casita Servin had shown me.

Just what I need, I thought: another house. I wasn't a land baron, just a writer with a bad case of wanderlust. Still, $200 a month was the price of a few meals out with friends in L.A., less than half what my writer friend James was paying to rent our casita in San Miguel. Servin was probably right that I'd save a little money by taking it. A point of departure for journeys into the region and beyond?

No, I didn't really need it. At first sight, the ruined garden and soft yellow walls had set off a tremor of delight—evoking the romance of youthful travels in southern Europe, probably, or student days when I lived only with books and ideas, presentiments and possibilities. Then there was the view of Citlaltépetl from the window over the desk.

A spot from which to consider the world anew. A place to plant my feet in between voyages as the world refigured itself around me.

I took out Gustavo's card and looked at it.

Mornings when I'm here, I wake up, walk outside, and ignite the pilot of the old *calentador*. Sometimes the drizzle, the *chipichipi*, extinguishes my Perla wax matches one by one, until finally, on my last strike, it lights. I brew a cup of indescribably strong coffee from nearby Coatepec and take it out into the ruined garden. There I lower myself into one of the rusted metal chairs, among the orchids and morning glories and broken walls, to wait for the shower water to heat up. I watch the sun burn away the mist, turning the casita walls a rich gold, illuminating the snowy volcanic peak; then, after a bow to the shade of Malcolm Lowry, I go inside for my shower.

12.

The Gringo Jarocho

I'd never heard of Raúl Pinkham Hellmer until I visited Tlacotalpan. But for a long time afterwards I couldn't get him out of my mind.

The Río Papaloapan, "river of butterflies" in the Nahua tongue, pours down from the Orizaba Mountains, merging with a tributary, the Río San Juan, just before emptying into the Caribbean, reaching a width of a thousand feet at the point where it passes the little town of Tlacotalpan. From an outdoor table at a *mariscos* restaurant on the *malecón*, nibbling *acamayas* (river shrimp) and sipping a *torito* (a drink of peanut, plum, and coconut), you can gaze across the silver-brown expanse to the far bank, or watch clumps of orchids, river birds perched on them, drift past in the languid air. Warm all year, furnace-hot in summer—though the river gives off the slightest of breezes, ventilating the town—Tlacotalpan is famously sweet, famously beautiful, famously romantic. *"Palmera y mujer . . . ,"* crooned

Agostín Lara, Mexico's great popular composer, invoking the region of his youth. The Mexican author Elena Poniatowska wrote: "Whenever we wish to smile, we think of Tlacotalpan."

On Gustavo Servin's advice, I headed down from Xalapa the weekend before the Fiesta de la Candelaria, the great yearly gathering of *son jarocho* musicians, to secure a room. If I didn't, he warned, I'd have to put up in nearby Alvarado or Cosamaloapan at best, as Tlacotalpan's two hotels were booked a year in advance. People rent out rooms in their houses for the weekend of the *feria*, he said. Just ask around.

Leaving Xalapa in a rented compact on a misty Friday morning, I emerged literally from a cloud onto the steep mountain road, the wide Veracruz plain spreading below. The air warmed quickly, and half an hour out of Xalapa the windows were open and I was down to a T-shirt. In some odd way, I felt released back into Mexico, which I always associate with warmth. The hour-long descent led through a succession of little towns, each with its gauntlet of spine-crunching, axle-busting *topes*—sudden humps in the road designed to slow traffic—that also fed the sellers of trinkets and snacks that congregated around them, and lined the pockets of waiting mechanics when a driver hit a tope too hard.

Reaching the flats, I skirted Veracruz City, host to its own upcoming carnival revels in a month, and bore south through villages of barefoot children and coconut palms until I caught my first whiff of salty Caribbean air. Merging with an oceanfront road, I followed signs pointing to Catemaco, a city known for its healers, *curanderos*, and sorcerers. This brought to mind a couple of gringas I knew back in San Miguel who always talked of visiting a *brujo* in Catemaco for *limpieza*, a cleansing, to deal with "some self-esteem issues," as they put it, but they never quite seemed to make it—a symptom, perhaps, of the condition they hoped to address. Or it might have been the recent advent of Simon, a self-styled British "shaman" who had "trained for six years in Chiapas," and his popular weekly San Miguel sweat lodges that had rendered their journey to Catemaco superfluous.

Passing Alvarado, a port town of fishermen, carpenters, and son jarocho musicians that still celebrates annually its defeat of invading U.S. military forces in 1846, I crossed a long toll bridge, then continued across the Papaloapan River delta, past lagoons, inlets, and clusters of snowy egrets. At the sign for Tlacotalpan I turned inland, following a flat riverside road that brought me in twenty minutes into the town.

Stepping out of my car at the wide central plaza, I realized I'd done myself a favor by coming a week early, for Tlacotalpan is truly beautiful, worth seeing uncrowded. Wide rectangular streets were laid out around a succession of interlocking plazas with Moorish kiosks, painted pavilions, gardens of exotic flowers, and white wrought-iron benches. The fantastical colors of the houses and buildings in variegated pastels—emerald, violet, lime green, pale pink, *rosa mexicano*, turquoise, yellow, melon, deep *azul*—were moderated by the lovely formalism of columns, colonnades, porticos, balconies, and floral patios. Elegant, ornately furnished living rooms opened to the street, crammed with potted palms and ferns, dim and beckoning, offering respite from the fierce sun. The aroma of cedarwood from carpenter shops filled the streets and plazas. There were few people about, and no visible signs of preparation for the festival to come.

Tlacotalpan's beauty bespoke its rich past: 549 historic edifices were identified by UNESCO when it declared it a World Heritage Site in 1998. The town struck me as a pocket version of old New Orleans or Havana—courtly, colorful, and defined above all by its music, for son jarocho is Tlacotalpan's jazz. And like those other Caribbean cities, both town and region were painted with the brush of African history and culture.

A Totonac pueblo founded sometime between A.D. 900 and 1200, Tlacotalpan was conquered by Montezuma in 1452. (Its name in Nahuatl means "half of the earth," referring to the confluence of two rivers. In the Mendocino Codex it appears in a hieroglyph represented as a circle, half black, half copper, with the symbols for cultivated earth.) Soon after the Spanish conquest, black slaves were sent here to work in sugar mills, ranchos, and fisheries. Sexual relations with Mesoamericans produced an Afro-mestizo people, with Spanish racial mixing as well. Rods used by brown-skinned and mulatto cowboys to drive cattle were known as *jarochas*, the men using them *jarochos*. By the nineteenth century jarochos were seen as a separate people with their own habits, laws, and special customs.

Ships crossing the Atlantic could enter the river estuary and debark at Tlacotalpan, picking up cotton, cedar, mahogany, tobacco, and various exotic tropical products, leaving behind luxuries from Europe and other ports in the Caribbean. By the early twentieth century, Tlacotalpan had a theater, a customs house, tram service, and public lighting. The decline in cotton production, and the advent of the train, ended its glory days; but Tlacotalpan's fall into decadence was gentle, the town preserved much as it was, its rich river delta culture intact.

Candelaria, or Candelmas, celebrations throughout Mexico mark the end of winter and the advent of spring, often with flowers and quiet religious ceremonies. Tlacotalpan's has different elements: a pagan bull run on Saturday; and on Sunday, the climactic river procession of an image of the Virgin, brought to Tlacotalpan by Andalusian sailors in the seventeenth century. Throughout the three-day festival, the *encuentro de jaranaros*—the biggest gathering of son jarocho and fandango music anywhere—draws visitors from all over Mexico and parts more distant.

I'd first encountered the music in the form sometimes called *huapango* or *huasteca*, from the regions of northern Veracruz and the Sierra Gorda. The tight guitars, the falsetto singing, the nimble lyrics and propulsive meters clearly stood apart from thumping Mexican mestizo music. It included a dance form, the elegant foot-stomping, flamenco-tinged fandango; and poetry, both in sung lyrics and in stand-alone *decimas*, ten-lined rhymed verses declaimed by its poets. Sometimes son jarocho was played with just the little guitars called *jaranas*, or with others called *requintos*, and at times with the addition of Veracruz harpists plucking shimmering single-note arpeggios. Whatever its form, the music had edge, imagination, and heat.

Most North Americans know son jarocho through the enduring Richie Valens rock and roll hit "La Bamba," originally a Veracruz song about a sailor—a staple of the idiom, still sung in endless lyric, rhythmic, and melodic variations. Its coursing eighth-note rhythm, looping melody, and spirit-lifting beat are typical of son jarocho. A music of great technical panache and spirit, it owes as much to Afro-Cubans who settled along this coast as to Spain and central Mexico. Played in villages and towns throughout Veracruz, son jarocho, in the hands of its masters, rises to sublime levels—comparable to southern Spain's flamenco, an early influence. And it is the African component that gives the music its distinctive élan and drive.

I could have spent the rest of the afternoon walking the quiet streets, poking into guitar shops, browsing in the Casa de la Cultura Agostín Lara, or drifting along the waterfront. But the heat was bearing down, the streets emptying for the hours of comida, and there remained the problem of finding a place to sleep the following weekend. At Doña LaLa, an old family-run hotel in the center of town, I asked if by chance they might still have a room. *"No, no hay,"* replied the capacious señora in the antique-filled lobby. She directed me to Tlacotalpan's other hotel, the Reforma. There the story was the same, but the reception clerk did write out the name of a woman, Lupita, with directions to her store, and suggested I ask there.

Crossing several plazas, I found Lupita's *tienda* beside a large, pretty church with a blue and white facade. She was in the back room, visible from the door, a large woman in a flower print dress, playing cards at a table with her teenage daughter. *"Sí, sí, hay,"* she called, rising to greet me.

I followed her to a simple one-story brick house a block away, behind the blue church. Several curs snoozed in the front yard. She led me into the shaded house and through a series of rooms to one in back, separated from the kitchen by a curtain. There were two beds with worn spreads, a single lamp, and a bed table. Old cartons and house supplies—cleansers, toilet paper, mops—were stacked along the walls. "These will be cleared away by next week," she said. "You can use the family bathroom and the kitchen." Her price—$60 for two nights—seemed stiff, but I had little appetite for more tromping around the deserted siesta streets in the blazing sun. Enraptured by Tlacotalpan, satisfied I'd at least secured a bed, I left Lupita a deposit and headed back to Xalapa.

For the next week, back in Xalapa's *zona de la niebla*, wherever I went—in cafés, taxis, markets—the radios were playing son jarocho alongside Ricky Martin and *ranchera* music. Even up here people knew Candelaria in Tlacotalpan was coming. El Agora, Xalapa's downtown cultural center, was selling posters for this year's *Encuentro de Jaraneras*, and I bought one and hung it in the little yellow casita beside the writing desk. On the advice of a taxi driver, I picked up a CD of the band Siquisiri and played it in my room along with Mono Blanco, a contemporary son jarocho group I'd seen perform in San Miguel. All week long, in the crumbling garden of the yellow house, I thought about Tlacotalpan. "*¡Qué vive y revive el son!*" sang Mono Blanco. *El son* lives—and lives again!

Early the following Friday I repeated the descent to the tropical coast. Arriving in Tlacotalpan in thickening traffic, I found my way back to Lupita's store, fetched the keys from her, and dropped my bags in the little room off the kitchen. The cartons and house supplies were still stacked along the walls, but one bed had been made up with clean sheets, and a bowl of fresh hibiscus in water decorated the table.

By late afternoon the plazas were filling with revelers. Music blared from loudspeakers, camera crews roamed. *Jaraneros* in their white *guayabera* shirts and distinctive small straw hats were tuning up along the street behind the Plaza Doña Marta, strumming licks, and laughing. A little after six, following upon some introductory words from the mayor of Tlacotalpan and a government official from Mexico City, a middle-aged man took the stage and began intoning a decima. Spoken slowly and gravely, often in praise of town or region, or the beauty of women, decimas, like Cuba's oral poetry, can be florid, ceremonial, or just plain corny; but the good poets wring from them high wit, irony, and biting social commentary. Over a thrumming carpet of sound provided by an eight-piece band, this decimista lauded Tlacotalpan, the fiesta, and the music of son jarocho, his last line drawing whoops and applause. Then the jaraneros took over with a pulsing song about life along the river, and the fiesta was under way.

In son jarocho, the singers' tight falsetto unleashes a coiled, poignant eroticism in love songs, a kind of strangled excitement in other songs of pleasure, a cock's crow of exultation. In duets sung with women, the similarities in pitch allow for different sorts of emotive interweaving. All this happens over a running current of strummed guitars and harps, with intermittent plucked guitar or harp solos—a form perfectly suited to story-telling.

It was a soft, sultry night beneath an ocean of stars and a swelling moon. As band after band lit up the plaza, people sat or stood or wandered in and out, ate tacos or ice cream, sipped cervezas or toritos. Not all the bands were good: one group from a village upriver had a lead singer of about twelve who sang painfully out of tune, the scraggly band accompanying him little better. Still, as the evening wore on, the bands got steadily better, and around nine o'clock a local group with a keening vocalist and a focused requinto soloist, who must have been seventy years old, had people on their feet, the wooden stage in the middle of the audience rattling with fandango dancers stomping out their stately, erect, furious steps.

Walking over to the thronged main square, I heard snatches of German, English, and Japanese among Spanish. A beautiful *zapateado*, the step-dance that is fandango, was in progress on the main stage, the men in white guayaberas, red scarves, and sombreros, feet flying. The straight-backed women, in white dresses, flowing black aprons, and rebozos, whirled like so many tops.

Back at the Plaza Doña Marta, during a break between bands, I was browsing a table of CDs for sale by the performing artists when I came upon one with a yellow cover and a lengthy title: *"A la trova más bonita de estos nobles cantadores . . . Grabaciones en Veracruz de José Raúl Hellmer."* To the most beautiful songs of these noble singers . . . Recorded in Veracruz by José Raúl Hellmer. The photo on the front showed three musicians in classic white garb and hats holding harp, jarana, and requinto. As much as I could tell without tearing off the cellophane, it looked to be an anthology, a collection of songs by various groups. I paid ninety pesos for it and stuck it in my shoulder bag.

The music started up again, with gusto: a passionate duet between a throaty woman and a delicate-voiced man singing a classic son jarocho love song, *"María Terolerolé."* Then a sharp-tongued young decimista worked into his lines some cutting allusions to the U.S. invasion of Afghanistan. A dance of *viejitos* followed, oldsters with canes doing sprightly fandangos. The bands would keep coming until dawn. Sometime around midnight, exhilarated and exhausted, I walked back to the little house, tiptoed to my room, and fell asleep.

I awoke to the sound of a toilet flushing, chatter in the kitchen. Light leaked through the curtain. I waited until it was quiet again, then dressed, washed up, and slipped out. It was a little after nine when I crossed the Plaza Doña Marta, deserted but for some dogs nosing through refuse from the festivities the night before. Along the streets by the river, crews were boarding up houses and laying chain link in preparation for the running of the bulls. In Hotel Doña LaLa's restaurant, sipping coffee among a few groggy breakfast customers nursing *crudas* (hangovers), I opened the CD package I'd bought the night before.

It had been put out recently by Conaculta, Mexico's national cultural institute, and contained nineteen examples of son jarocho field recordings, collected over forty years by one José Raúl Hellmer. A twenty-eight-page brochure was inset into the sleeve. I slid it out and opened it.

On the first page a geeky-looking gringo if I ever saw one gazed out from a black and white photo. He wore large, round plastic-rimmed glasses, his hair standing up in a thick clump like Barton Fink's, dressed in khaki clothes of a 1950s cut. He had a large tanned face with a long jaw and thick lips. Lean, tall it would appear, he looked to be somewhere in his late thirties. A small box camera hung from a strap around his neck, a couple of pens clipped to his shirt pocket. He was leaning against a wall, some Mexican town in the background, gazing toward the horizon with an earnest, dedicated expression. The photo reeked of an era—a metaphysic, even. Everything about it said "field trip."

On the page opposite the photo, a text began in Spanish, entitled *"El Gringo Jarocho."*

It told how Joseph Ralph (José Raúl) Pinkham Hellmer had been born in Philadelphia in 1913 and, attracted in youth to Eastern philosophies, had had an early premonition of his life's calling: to create brotherhood through music. Coming across a stack of old son jarocho records in a bin, he experienced an epiphany, a total identification of some sort. In 1946 he arrived in Mexico to begin what was to be his life's work: researching and collecting Mexican folklore. He became, the notes said, "one of the most prolific investigators of Mexican music, marked by the search for a human horizon at the margins of the bellicosity that characterized the first half of the twentieth century, a search that had touched him in his very flesh."

Turning the page, I came upon a second photo of Hellmer, a little bit older, wearing the same round plastic glasses, dressed now like a jarocho himself in a white outfit and a Veracruz hat, still with the pens in his pocket. He was walking beside the ocean, carrying a jarana guitar, a soft smile on his face.

In the pages that followed, a former Mexican colleague recalled Hellmer's passion for his work: Hellmer in Tlacotalpan recording fandangos and serenades; the chants of roosters, bells, birds; the mysterious noises of the Río Papaloapan; the morning itself. Hellmer in the foothills of the Pico de Orizaba, capturing some village requinto player on tape, submerged in an ecstatic, sensuous trance; Hellmer trying to eternalize a moonlit night with his box camera. "This was José Raúl Pinkham Hellmer, the gringo jarocho," the essayist wrote, "a man who savored every instant, and when it came to the music of the Gulf, a relentless sybarite."

It was easy to picture Hellmer, headphones on, checking the dials on his reel-to-reel portable Nagra, then closing his eyes in rapture as he recorded Rutilio Parroquín, El Zapateado, the great early singer and jarana player, upriver in Otatitlán, where pilgrims come every year to worship the Black Christ.

Alan Lomax in the Mississippi Delta, recording Leadbelly

and Robert Johnson. Harry Smith in the Appalachias. Folk-
ways, Nonesuch Records, the Smithsonian anthologies. *The
Family of Man.* Passionate, idealistic Americans—musicologists,
anthropologists, writers, filmmakers—aroused and disgusted
by two world wars, armed with notebooks, recording devices,
and a sincere interest in the people and cultures of the world,
setting out to build bridges among tribes and nations. If we
could but understand each other better, surely we could turn
swords into plowshares! The United Nations Charter. The
Declaration of Human Rights. The Peace Corps. Freedom Rid-
ers. I thought of the writers and filmmakers who had gone out
then too: Alan Watts and Gary Snyder to Japan; Paul Bowles to
Morocco; Allen Ginsberg to India; the filmmaker Maya Deren
to Haiti. Like Joseph Ralph Hellmer, they went not to convert
but to be converted: to sit patiently at the feet of a rough field
hand with a guitar, or an indigenous storyteller, or a guru; to listen, watch, record, take notes. Cultural voyagers, seeking a path
away from conflict and misunderstanding, seeking revelation in
cultures not their own—even as forces in Washington and elsewhere were setting the world on a harder, more cynical, course.
Their heartfelt documentations yielded treasures we draw upon
daily.

Reading on in the CD brochure, I came to a third photo of
Hellmer, his glasses black-rimmed now, the lenses thicker, his
steel wool hair jutting up intact. He sat in a chair, legs crossed,
strumming a jarana and singing, against what appears to be a
painted scrim of a palm tree and a moon—probably some Mexico City television studio. He looked older, crustier, strained.

Opposite the photo was a statement in quotes, in Spanish: "My personality isn't important for the moment, but I tell people that I am an ex-gringo from Philadelphia—my friends tell me that I am a Veracruzano, born by accident in the United States—who has more than a half century of age and twenty-two years in Mexico struggling for the cause of folklore. I've made more than six hundred programs for radio and television. But now I feel confused, with so many obstacles in the system of education, so deficient in its formative aspects, and in the consequent confusion in the minds of ordinary people with respect to the true goals of man . . ."

This quote was dated August 25, 1967. Four years later Raúl Hellmer would be dead in Mexico City at fifty-seven, his ashes scattered off the Veracruz coast by family and friends.

In the restaurant of the Hotel Doña LaLa, staring at the photo of this ardent investigator, this gringo jarocho, my chest filled with sorrow. Here we were again, trapped in the same morass of "bellicosity." We'd gone nowhere, learned nothing, it seemed.

In 1967, the year of Hellmer's quote, "folk music" was becoming a dead issue in his home country. Black blues had been co-opted by commercial rock and roll. Dylan had gone electric. The growing war in Vietnam darkened the horizon. The following year protesting students would be mowed down in Mexico City and elsewhere in the world. New currents were sweeping away quaint folklorists like Raúl Hellmer, castigated as sentimental liberals, their preservationist battles a lost cause. Identity politics would discredit the act of empathy with other cultures, assuming the mantle of voices not your own, as just a game of patronizing white men. And how many times had the music turned over since Hellmer's day? Pop, punk, hip-hop . . .

The sudden entry of a son jarocho group into Doña Lala's brought me out of my bleak reverie. Dressed in white, they began serenading the tables with an electrifying, rouse-the-dead "La Bamba" that all but rendered coffee superfluous, the harpist's staccato solo lifting the hairs on the back of my neck.

Back outside, sun was warming the Tlacotalpan streets. More buildings had been fenced off for the bull run. The tempo of the weekend was picking up. Today would be all about beer, whooping, and blood. Nobody would care about son jarocho, much less the spectral memory of Raúl Pinkham Hellmer. Reaching the Plaza Doña Marta, I thought how discouraged Hellmer sounded in that final quote, that people couldn't seem to recognize the glories of their own culture. It was as true now as then: Mexicans, like everybody else, wanted their MTV. Hellmer's dream had been swatted away by history's cold hand.

But was that really true? I sat down on a bench in the empty plaza where last night there'd been barely a place to stand or sit for the singing, playing, and dancing. Tlacotalpan's Fiesta de la Candelaria celebrated a huge resurgence in the music Hellmer had loved, among players and listeners from the region and far beyond. In truth, people everywhere played and listened to one another's music far more than in Hellmer's day, if shorn of its socialist idealism. In Xalapa I hadn't been able to get into El Agora's movie theater to see *The Buena Vista Social Club*; tickets were sold out for the week. Nusrat Fatah Ali Khan,

Ladysmith Black Mambazo, Baba Mal, Caetano Veloso, Lila Downs: cross-cultural dialogues, sampling, and mixing. Maybe expecting the world's music to stanch human "bellicosity" was demanding too much.

That afternoon, while the bull run raged, I drove upriver for a while in my rented car. Popping Hellmer's anthology into the dashboard CD player, I listened as glimpses of the Río Papaloapan, cradle of son jarocho music, flickered past through the palms. Some of the nineteen selections sounded squeaky, antique, the sort of stuff only an aficionado could appreciate; others sounded as fresh as tomorrow, ripping out of the speakers, and would have easily commanded the stage at the Doña Marta. I eased back into Tlacotalpan at siesta hour as the last song played, *"La Lloroncita,"* by an old group from Boca Del Rio.

The Plaza Doña Marta was jammed that night, the bands even better, the fandango stomping intense. Watching a young Japanese NHK crew crouched down in front with digital cameras and mikes as Mono Blanco played an old song Raúl Hellmer would surely have known, I kept seeing his ghost hovering on the fringes of the crowd, in his geeky glasses and khaki outfit, pens in his pocket, a blissful smile on his face. *"¡Qué vive y revive el son!"*

Sunday morning at dawn I walked through deserted Tlacotalpan to the river. A mist hung over the Río Papaloapan. Water lapped against the jetties. A lone oarsman stood at the back of a pirogue. He beckoned, and I jumped in. The pale light of daybreak spread up from the gulf behind us as we rode silently upriver, hugging the shore, past mangroves and reeds and old ruined riverfront villas from the time when the Atlantic ships had docked here and the town had been rich. Listening to river sounds and bird calls, I imagined Hellmer holding his microphone out, trying to keep his equipment dry, recording all this. How a person's passions can overtake him utterly! The music of son jarocho had lured Ralph Hellmer far from his culture of origin, echoing some alienation or displacement already in him, leading him to seek inspiration, and a home, elsewhere. In what is our identity truly rooted? The wayfaring stranger. Who among us is not one?

The silent rower crossed the swift current, drawing abreast of an island in the middle of the river. Then as he turned back toward shore, Tlacotalpan spread before us in profile, first sunlight tipping the church spires. In a few hours the river would become the site of Candelaria's climactic event, the Paseo de la Virgin. Already a mass was under way, the jaraneros gathering in church to sing her *"Las Mañanitas,"* the Mexican birthday song, and *"La Llorona,"* the weeping woman. Then the Virgin would be carried to the *malecón* and put onto a barge. Thousands would throng to the river to try and take the trip with her. Tonight the Plaza Doña Marta would ring again with son jarocho.

Onshore, I walked back to Lupita's and started to pack my bags.

"¿Cómo le va, señor?"

I turned around. Lupita's wide frame filled the doorway.

"*Bien,*" I said. "*Muy bien.*"

"You slept well?"

"Yes."

"You're not at the river to see the Virgin."

No, I said, I wouldn't be staying today to see it all. I'd gotten what I'd come for, and more.

She looked surprised. Then she just smiled, shrugged, and said, "*Ni modo.*" Whatever.

The colored walls and plazas flashed past on the road out of Tlacotalpan, echoing with sounds of fandango and son jarocho. I turned east toward the Caribbean and drove into the sun.

13.

Katanchel: Sacha's Honeymoon

N*o es un hotel, es un sueño."*

A scruffy, blinkered burro drew the little wooden trolley along a path cut through the Mayan jungle toward the bungalow where I was to stay. The words of Aníbal González, architect-owner of Hacienda Katanchel, no matter how often he might have spoken them, seemed directed to me alone. As we bumped across the grounds of this resurrected seventeenth-century hacienda in the afternoon hush, Katanchel really did seem less a hotel than a dream.

I'd never had a burning yen to visit resort hotels, especially secluded tropical ones. Expensive and over-heavy on concept, they promised inescapable communion with the very sorts one hoped to avoid by traveling. The prospect of encountering the same diners meal after meal filled me not with pleasure but dread. Being tended to by indigenous people obliged to market their patrimony to foreigners made me uncomfortable. Designer sybaritism; theme parks in miniature; stationary cruise ships; retirement communities in rehearsal. No, a friend had said, Katanchel is something different. You'll see.

I'd arrived in the Yucatán the day before from Mexico City, the descent through cloud cover revealing peninsular forest stretching to the blue Caribe, broken only by an occasional village or the tip of a Mayan ruin. In graceful, melancholy Mérida, the state capital, I'd walked the twilit colonial streets among slow men in guayabera shirts and women in sleeveless dresses. I'd dined on toothsome *puuc chuc*, the regional pork specialty smothered in red onions and sour oranges, and in my downtown hotel room listened to a Mayan quartet whack out "Proud Mary" in a lounge off the plant-clotted courtyard. I'd fallen asleep with James Lloyd Stephens's 1843 classic, *Incidents of Travel in Yucatan*, with Frederick Catherwood's haunting drawings of Mayan ruins, on my chest, awakened only briefly around midnight to the Eagles' "Lyin' Eyes" drifting up from below.

In the morning I'd walked in light rain to Mérida's grand central market in search of sisal hammocks, once a staple of the region. I'd found an old man selling some and bought four: one for the roof in San Miguel, one for the ruined garden in Xalapa, a couple as gifts. Then I'd driven a rented Nissan south a half hour, toward the ancient Mayan city-complex of Chichén Itzá, before turning east onto a muddy trail at a small wooden sign that said simply KATANCHEL.

The mule trolley rocked beneath green, dripping fronds, past glistening pools and low-surfaced adobe cabins painted oxblood red—few occupied, it seemed. Aníbal Gonzáles, as he explained himself, was a Spanish architect who had been living in Mexico City with his wife, Mónica Hernández, described in the hotel's brochure as an archaeologist and botanist, elsewhere as an art restorer and expert in reforestation. They'd come upon this 741-acre sisal, or henequen rope, plantation, abandoned in the 1950s when the invention of nylon rendered the sisal industry nearly obsolete, and bought it in 1995. The word *Katanchel* in ancient Mayan means, depending upon where you read it, "where the Milky Way passes over" or "where one asks the arc of the sky." An astronomical observatory dating from the third century A.D. was under excavation just off the road leading back to the highway.

Hopping off at the last bungalow before unmediated jungle, I stood alone in the earth-walled entry garden of the cabin that was to be mine for the next two nights. Shivering bromeliad leaves spilled raindrops. The damp air seemed to breathe with me. A ring of black butterflies danced around the lintel above the screen door. Frogs murmured; then the whoop of some wild bird soloed out from a tapestry of sound receding to some vanishing point in deep forest.

Inside, the bungalow basked in light. A canopied cast-iron bed floated on a terra-cotta tile floor. Dresser, chairs, mirrors, and a desk of carved tropical wood and rattan stood framed against rose-washed walls. Simple, elegant, arranged without imposing, the high-ceilinged room was silent but for ambient forest sounds. A door out back led to a small plunge pool fed by mineral spring water, the nearest bungalow obscured by foliage.

"No es un hotel, es un sueño."

How different those words sound today, knowing what I know. I retain especially, against what would befall Katanchel, that sweet moment of arrival.

Resisting the urge to peel off my clothes and sink into the pool, I decided instead to explore the grounds before dark. I took a path leading away from the hotel deeper into the jungle, coming after a while to a gate marking the end of the development. Just beyond, a small community of Mayans, attached to Katanchel somehow I assumed, greeted me as I passed. Taking a different route through the forest back to the resort, I passed cultivated gardens and orchards, windmill-driven wells, bird-watching towers, ruined walls and gates that must have belonged to the old plantation. Built during the 1600s on the grounds of an ancient Mayan settlement, Katanchel was one of many Spanish land-grant ranches in the Yucatán originally devoted to raising cattle introduced from Spain to the Americas. But it was the nineteenth-century boom in the cultivation of the *Agave sisalana* cactus, processed into rope fiber, that brought enormous wealth to the region.

At dusk, I emerged near the main building, the old central hacienda, with its wide, terraced *entrada* and massive rooms serving these days as reception area, library, and lounge. Skirting a gazebo nestled among palms, I came to the main swimming pool, its indigo waters reflecting candles already lit. Just beyond it lay the old sisal factory, called the Casa de Máquinas, retooled by Aníbal González into Katanchel's restaurant.

I was the first diner, seated alone in the soaring building among a dozen tables on a raised polished wooden floor, open to the jungle on three sides. Ceiling fans circled far overhead. A spectacular site for a restaurant, if a little unnerving to eat staring into the impenetrable dark where jaguars depicted in Mayan friezes once roamed, happy to make a meal of you. It was the first moment I felt something quixotic, vulnerable about Katanchel.

The menu offered imaginative dishes made from ingredients grown in the hacienda gardens, with fresh-baked bread from the neighboring village of Tixkokob and fish from coastal Telchac, twenty-five miles away. Other diners began arriving— a young Mexican couple who looked to be newlyweds; a trio of middle-aged academics, I guessed. Katanchel, I'd read, often hosted archaeologists, ornithologists, ecologists, and botanists alongside those who more commonly found their way to luxury resorts. The owners, Aníbal and Mónica, appeared, greeting each table of guests in turn. After we'd talked briefly about the wonders of Katanchel, they joined another arriving couple for dinner.

While I ate a dish of peppers stuffed with seafood, I leafed through the hotel's promotional brochure:

> You can dine to Mozart, drink brandy while admiring 17th century artifacts in the Grand Salon, and discover the remains of an ancient Mayan settlement in the hotel grounds. With over a dozen optional expert-guided cultural and nature excursions, there is no shortage of things to do. Or if you prefer to simply unwind, laze by the pool or try the blissful organic

honey and flower petal body mask, just one of the natural spa treatments on offer.

Standard tourist spiel, probably written by some PR firm. I sensed in the Gonzálezes, bright with aesthetic and ecological idealism, a struggle to fit their private labor of love into the frame of modern resort marketing, when their real passions lay in architecture and archaeology. So far I was persuaded they'd managed to fashion a tasteful, sensitive, self-sufficient Eden, a multifaceted "nature resort," free of the onerous conditions Mayans had once endured on these rope plantations. Still, there was that hint of "the jungle experience," packaged:

> The Tienda de Raya (the name for the traditional hacienda on-premise general store and wage payment center) has become a spacious lounge, library, office, and boutique featuring Maya crafts. Meeting venues are available from ballroom to classroom formats.

The young newlyweds sat close together over their *pollo en pipián* and champagne, hands locked beneath the table, gazing into each other's eyes by candlelight to the frog opera from the great dark wall of jungle beyond. Exotic, reclusive, and beautiful, Hacienda Katanchel was also wildly romantic.

Just before leaving for the Yucatán, I'd heard that Sacha, a painter friend in New York, had become engaged and was planning to marry later that year. He was looking for a honeymoon spot. Did I have any recommendations? At my table in the Casa de Máquinas, savoring a dessert of *ciricote*, a local fruit I'd never heard of let alone tasted, I was certain I'd found the perfect spot.

The path back to my bungalow led through a grassy field lit by starlight so strong it was easy to see why Mayan astronomers had chosen this site to "track the heavenly progress of the gods," in the brochure's phrase. The only sound was the surging of frogs, the lone visible movement darting bat shadows.

In the bungalow bed, immured in a cocoon of mosquito netting, I opened another of the books I'd brought with me. I began to read how in the burnt-out last days of World War II, a young Russian soldier, rummaging through the ruins of the Berlin Library, had come across surviving fragments of Mayan texts. Spiriting them back to his apartment in Leningrad, he began trying to decipher them. The mystery of Mayan inscriptions, inscribed in stone on temples and set down in books known as codices, went back as far as the Conquest. During the settling and attendant pillaging of the Maya at the hands of the Spaniards, most Mayan writing was destroyed—notably during the Spanish bishop Diego de Landa's infamous book burnings in Maní, a town not far from where I lay—and the few surviving codices had been removed to various European museums. James Lloyd Stephens, during his travels in the early eighteenth century, had found forty-three separate Mayan cities, overgrown and unexcavated, and had been one of the first to suggest that indigenous Americans—not Egyptians, Greeks, Atlanteans, or one of the lost tribes of Israel—might have built the great pyramids and temples, and that they were the remains of a single remarkable civilization.

As the magnitude of the Mayans' attainments in building, science, and the arts became incontrovertibly clear, and with the decipherment of ancient Egypt's hieroglyphs and the Rosetta Stone in hand, decoding Mayan writing became the great archaeological and linguistic grail. Several generations of scholars in Mexico, Europe, and the United States undertook expeditions and studies, asserting a variety of theories about the construction and meaning of Mayan texts. But it was Yuri Knorosov, the former Russian soldier, working in Cold War obscurity in Leningrad, never having traveled to the Americas, who puzzled out the fact that Mayan writing combined both syllabic sounds and word symbols, or logograms. Armed with this new knowledge, linguists began unraveling the inscriptions, discovering that the message in the glyphs was neither metaphysical nor religious, as most leading scholars had staked their careers upon asserting, but an elaborate dated record of successions of kings and dynasties. The Maya, it emerged, were a deeply religious, stratified, warlike culture, rooted in mathematics and astronomy.

It was this vivid tale of scholarly sleuthing, recounted in Michael Coe's *Breaking the Maya Code*, that I read that night in the bungalow at Katanchel. My visit to the Yucatán, as befit my brief from the travel magazine, was to spend a few nights at the hacienda and take a quick look at Mérida today; but to me it was the prelude to another journey to southern Mexico a month hence to join my friend David Lebrun, shooting a film based upon Coe's book at ancient Mayan sites.

Reading deep into the night, serenaded by the sudden whoops and caws of forest creatures, I felt far from the contemporary world yet connected to it along some deeper wheel of time, where human splendors crumbled into ruins: Landa and his burning books, Knorosov in burning Berlin, Stephens and Catherwood among the buried Mayan cities. We live like hermit crabs, I thought, inside the crumbling exoskeletons, the abandoned dreams of those who came before. While "experts" poke among the rubble of the World Trade Center for clues, my country destroys what was already destroyed in Afghanistan in order to evict the Taliban, who in their brief reign annihilated venerable Buddha statues. Now Iraq, cradle of civilization, rich with irreplaceable ruins and treasures, lies in our bomber sights. Tonight I will sleep beside the buried site of an ancient observatory, where Mayan priest-scientists once sought to read some greater order in the heavens.

The next day, after an early breakfast in the Casa de Máquinas of *motuleños*—fried eggs, beans, diced ham, peas, onions, fried tortillas, and fried bananas—I left Katanchel and headed south to Chichén Itzá, hoping to beat the tourists. A decade had passed since I'd last been there. On that trip Masako and I had landed at Cancún airport just long enough to rent a car, then driven several hours south to visit an old poet friend, Toni Gérez, who had built a *palapa* with thatch roof and no walls—her *na*, as she called it, using the Mayan name—on a stretch of jungle beach south of Tulum, the onetime Mayan fortress and trading port. We'd cooked meals in her outdoor oven, slept in hammocks cooled by sea breeze, and the next day driven to the inland excavation site at Cobá, most of its 6,500 structures still covered by jungle, and climbed among the ruins. Continuing across the peninsula, we'd spent a day at Chichén Itzá, the vast Mayan-Toltec city and ceremonial site that had been abandoned centuries before the Spaniards came. Though I'd since visited other Mayan sites in southern Mexico and Guatemala—kingdoms once stretching unbroken from the Yucatán to Honduras—the impact of Chichén's sprawling grandeur had stayed with me.

Pulling into the parking lot, I realized I'd arrived too late. It was a Sunday, at the height of the tourist season, and since my last visit Chichén had become a full-blown Yucatecan Disneyland, with gift shops, fast-food restaurants, a slide-show auditorium, and currency exchange. Elbowing through the turnstiles among noisy Mexican and foreign families in shorts and T-shirts, I felt skinless, fragile after the intimate embrace of Katanchel and the jungle. El Castillo, the monumental central pyramid and calendar in stone, with its 365 stairs and plumed serpent tracking the equinoxes, was a swarming human termitarium. The enigmatic, reclining statue of Chac Mool, the Mayan rain god, was obscured by visitors taking snapshots. Hordes roamed the ball courts where once, among fantastical inscriptions of fertility worship, the game was played to the death.

I hurried back to my car in the scorching midday sun. Speeding back down the highway in air-conditioned cool, I tried to reason more calmly. Was it so bad, the marketing of the early Mayas' brilliance for the economic benefit of their descendants? A tourist-filled Chichén Itzá probably more resembled the original city than the empty province of archaeologists, adventurers, and artists I'd have wished for.

I'd planned to go on to Mérida for lunch and look up some young Mexican artists working there; but instead I turned back down the dirt path to Katanchel, eager to spend my remaining afternoon and night among its leafy, dappled mysteries, in the sheltered safety and calm of the jungle.

The following morning at four I arose and padded through pitch-black to my car. Headlights carved the deserted highway road to the airport and an early flight to Mexico City.

As soon as I got back to Xalapa, I e-mailed Sacha in New York. "I've found the perfect place for your honeymoon," I effused, going on to sing Hacienda Katanchel's praises. I closed with Aníbal's phrase: *"No es un hotel, es un sueño."*

The first indication that something was wrong came later that year, in the form of an e-mail, dated November 4, entitled *"Ayuda para Katanchel"* (Help for Katanchel) from Mónica Hernández González, the archaeologist/botanist wife of Aníbal. Katanchel continued without electricity, she wrote in Spanish, but what was even worse, the houses of the ninety-five workers didn't have roofs. She and her staff were very concerned with the reconstruction of Hacienda Katanchel, and struggling with the insurance company to give them the money owed. The estimate for reparations of the houses was 1 million pesos (about $100,000). This news was followed by a request for aid and a routing number for a bank account in Mérida, where tax-deductible donations could be sent in the name of Pronatura Península de Yucatán, a conservation agency associated with the World Wildlife Fund.

I immediately wrote Sacha. The last I'd heard, they'd been leaning toward a Katanchel honeymoon. Did he know anything?

His answer came the next day.

After the wedding, followed by a reception boat trip around the island of Manhattan in perfect late September weather, he and his new bride, Angela, had flown to Mérida, where they were picked up and driven to Katanchel. "That night," he wrote, "we frolicked like excited children in our jungle hideaway, crowded in by the noise of cicadas and frogs, the bizarre sense of all that wilderness between us and the smiling wedding party."

The next day they heard from an assistant manager at Katanchel—Aníbal and Mónica were vacationing in Europe—that a hurricane was coming through from Cuba. It was tracking north of the peninsula and would probably blow itself out in the gulf, they were told. "The worst we would get would be a few days of rain. I relaxed. It was rainy season, after all."

The following day the honeymooners spent disporting themselves, in love with each other and now with Hacienda

Katanchel. Then, Sacha wrote, "after a deep sleep we woke to a white, cloud-bound sky. I had brought watercolors so we sat on the terrace and did some painting. I tried a jungle view but couldn't fix the light. The sky was pulsing white and blue. Then it deepened to a greenish, lead-gray and exploded in a tropical downpour. We were elated; we'd never seen rain like this. Angela scampered out in her bikini and did a Mary Tyler Moore in the sparkling torrent. After a long hot summer in Harlem we were thirsty for this. We hurried to the pool and jumped in. Underwater, the surface sizzled with rain. I came up in the choking downpour and lay on the side of the pool, arms open to the sky, letting the rain scour and cleanse away my tensions."

But the rain didn't stop.

"By next morning we were beginning to tire of the constant onslaught. At breakfast the jungle shifted wearily in the wet wind. At a nearby table three English guests played cards." They attempted a trip into Mérida but found everything closed, windows taped up, managing to make it back to Katanchel by removing trees that had fallen over the jungle road. Sacha logged onto the hotel's Internet service.

"What I saw made my mouth fall open. Swirling over the Yucatán, in angry reds and yellows, was the enormous form of Isidore, eight hundred miles across—enough cloud and wind to swallow up the Gulf of Mexico. The eye was currently just off the north coast of the Yucatán, as we had been told, but the winds we were experiencing seemed to indicate that the storm was either stronger than predicted or was actually moving in our direction."

Struggling back to their cabin in gale winds, they latched the wooden shutters and "lay on the bed, hugging each other as the howling increased around us." The jungle came crashing down. The bungalow was plunged in darkness as the electricity failed. They remained trapped there until two Mayans came: " 'The animals . . . they will come in from the jungle . . . you must come.' "

For the next two days and nights while Hurricane Isidore raged, reaching Level Four with winds of 145 miles per hour, Sacha and Angela camped out inside the four-hundred-year-old main building with the other guests and Mayans who worked at Katanchel, eating what they could find. The storm had torn the roof off the bar and the restaurant; the kitchen was flooded, most of the food spoiled. The Yucatán had been declared a disaster area, the airport closed. The army was dropping supplies; President Vicente Fox was due to visit the region the next day.

On the third day, the storm having been "downgraded to a blustery drizzle," they went back to their bungalow. They found the veranda torn away, the shutters blown open, the floor flooded, the bathroom roof gone, and the corridor "an open grave of smashed tiles and broken beams." In the restaurant, the Casa de Máquinas, the roof was torn open, dining tables chopped in half by fallen beams, ceiling fans relieved of their blades. "In the kitchen, flies buzzed over an abandoned pot of beans. Glass refrigerators were fogged by perishing food."

In the Grand Salon ("where you can dine to Mozart, drink brandy while admiring 17th century artifacts") "all the fake columns and cupolas had been ripped open to reveal a paltry skeleton of twisted aluminium. The roof was all sky. A massive cake of rubble sat on the sofa where I had leafed through a magazine only two nights before."

The road out remained impassable, all communications with the outside cut. In his journal Sacha wrote: "I have no idea if our families know about this. I almost hope they don't because I can't get word to them that we're alive. Happy honeymoon, dude."

That night, unable to stand the thought of another night cooped up in the hacienda, he and Angela went looking for a dry bungalow in torrential rain. They'd been in the same wet clothes for two days and were desperate for a warm, dry bed. All forty bungalows had been flooded or destroyed. Eventually they picked one and "set to work sweeping out the water and towel-drying it. Angela lit some candles and slipped on her wedding nightie." They spent the night there among buzzing mosquitoes, "as floodwater had overwhelmed their control pools and they now had ample opportunity to breed," inviting dengue fever.

Finally, despite continuing heavy rain, workers managed to clear the road enough for them to try to leave. "On the terrace, the Mayans were gathered around a steaming pot of beans. We moved among them, trying to make our gratitude felt. Their villages were rubble, their wives and children sat huddled in exposed tenements, but they had trudged in from the jungle to save us. Angela wept at the sight of these magnificent men."

Driving to the airport in shell-shocked silence, through evidence of the storm's destruction everywhere, they knew it would take years for the Yucatán to repair itself. At the airport crowds of people were struggling to get out; there would be no flights until the next day.

Sacha and Angela flew to Mexico City, hoping to distance themselves from the trauma for the few days left of their honeymoon before returning to New York. "But the storm hung around our necks. We couldn't shake it.

"All I know," Sacha ended, "is that on my honeymoon the earth moved, there was an excess of passion; and my wife and I emerged from a destroyed paradise, hand in hand."

Hacienda Katanchel announced plans to reopen in 2003, but as of summer 2005 it remained closed. Recently I tried to e-mail Mónica Hernández González and received back "Returned mail: User unknown." Hacienda Katanchel's e-mail address kicked back the same.

Weirdly, hauntingly—and this may say something about the Internet and how it functions, what persists and what dies, and how information outlives the realities it describes—when I did an Internet search, the first entries brought up the same sites promoting Katanchel as three years before, including Katanchel's own website, with the online version of the brochure I'd read at dinner in the Casa de Máquinas that night: "You can dine to Mozart, drink brandy while admiring 17th century artifacts in the Grand Salon . . ."

Out there in cyberspace, time had stood still; nothing had

happened in the Yucatán that September 2002. The other travel reservation sites, scores of them, still invited you to book a bungalow at a hotel that had ceased to exist. Hacienda Katanchel was still the paradise it had been, not what it had in fact become: a ruin among ruins.

"No es un hotel, es un sueño." Not a hotel but a dream.

14.

To Palenque

Villahermosa, seen from an Aeromexico window seat on descent, looks to be as lovely as its name. Set in a rich green expanse of jungle veined with lagoons, near the Gulf Coast in the southwestern corner of the Yucatán Peninsula, it clusters along the banks of the wide, winding Río Grijalva. But it is a city of commerce, overrun by oil development, and is not pretty at all. Its main attractions are La Venta, a museum and park with huge al fresco Olmec heads; its anthropology museum; and its position as a gateway to Palenque, my destination.

As far as I knew, my filmmaker friend David and his crew had been at Palenque for five days, shooting the great ruins and inscriptions there. They had three left to go, days I hoped to spend with them. After long preparation, they'd begun shooting *Breaking the Maya Code* two weeks earlier at Mexico City's anthropology museum, among its peerless Mayan collection. Their two-month shoot would take them deep into southeastern Mexico, Guatemala, and Honduras. Like me, they'd flown to Villa-hermosa; then after a day's shooting at La Venta they'd moved on to Palenque. Or so I assumed: I hadn't had any contact with them since they'd left the States. An e-mail I'd sent several days earlier had gone unanswered. I was going on faith that they were there, and that we'd meet as planned.

Stepping off the plane into tropical mid-afternoon heat, I entered the small terminal and found the Hertz counter. A pretty Mayan woman in a white blouse walked me across the parking lot to a large silver-toned, four-door car called a Tstratus. I'd never heard of a Tstratus, which looked like a generic Detroit model, but she presented it as a stroke of good fortune—in effect, a free upgrade instead of the economy model I'd reserved. When it took five tries to open the trunk with the remote button on the key ring, I decided to stash my luggage instead in the backseat. The car was pimpled with dents and dings; inside, the odometer read a suspicious 13,000 miles; the gas gauge hovered just above empty. The nearest Pemex station, she said, was around a *glorieta*, over a *puente*, and across the highway.

Pulling out of the parking lot, I was immediately swept onto a four-lane highway, past a sign said CHETUMAL PALENQUE. It looked from the map to be a straight run of about 130 kilometers to the Palenque turnoff, then a short drive from there—a journey of about two hours, depending upon road and traffic. The odometer now read 93,000 miles: 13,000 must have been the trip reading, then, not the overall miles. Had the previous renter taken a 13,000-mile trip around Mexico? The rattling Tstratus seemed to answer "yes."

After ten minutes or so, no glorieta or puente or Pemex had appeared, the gas gauge had settled firmly on E, and I began to experience a sensation I didn't like. At the next *retorno*, I slowed on squishy, squealy brakes and headed back toward Villahermosa.

Streaming past the airport toward the city center, I spotted a Pemex on the other side and pulled in.

"*Lleno con Magna,*" I told the *gasolinero*.

"*No hay,*" he said.

"How far is it to the next station?"

"Forty-two kilometers."

"Do you have Premium?"

"*Sí.*"

I asked him if the Tstratus would function on the high-octane gas, which cost nearly twice as much.

"I suppose," he said.

"*Lleno con Premium.*"

With a full tank and shrinking confidence in the Tstratus, I headed back in the direction of Palenque. The flat green Yucatán Peninsula stretched ahead, a quilt of maize, sorghum, and squash farms, grazing white oxen, sheep, and small pale horses. To my right, the low foothills of the Sierra de Chiapas sloped up to a cloud-checkered sky.

The road soon narrowed to two lanes, traffic slowing to the lowest common denominator. Sandwiched among trucks and buses, I rode the Tstratus's spongy, protesting brakes. As space in oncoming traffic appeared, cars pulled out to pass—on uphill grades, in disregard of double lines or curves ahead, sometimes directly in the face of approaching cars. A nervous flurry followed on both sides as cars tried to sneak back across the line just before provoking one of those head-on, multicar crashes featured in the pages of Mexican dailies, often warranting a pull-out section of their own called *Policiaca* or *Crimenes*, full of grisly accidents, murders, and abductions.

My fitful passage to Palenque, with its slows, sprints, and near-misses, was soon complicated by the inevitable appearance of *topes*, those humps in the road designed to slow traffic, also known as *vibradores* or *reductores de velocidad* in regions where people bothered to post warning signs. But *topes* is what everyone knows them by, and the road to Palenque was full of them. Even the most vigilant driver tackling a new stretch of Mexican road will crash at least one tope at high speed. This tests the mettle—and the metal—of the car, as well as the driver's spine and internal organs, and the headroom of the car's cabin. I'd finally managed to pass a long smoky line of buses and trucks when a tope appeared out of nowhere. I slammed on the brakes to great squealing and little slowing, then bounced over the tope, my butt separating from the seat, my head grazing the cabin roof. As the smell of burning brakes filled the cab, I saw the kids who sell bags of *jícama* by the tope laughing their heads off.

From there on I simply dawdled behind whichever lumbering dirt truck or rickety *camion* full of live pigs happened to be ahead, letting green *campo* slide by, cursing the car and the agency for giving me this bucket of bolts, until I reached the Palenque turnoff. From there, bearing westward, I ascended along a road that, were I to continue on it, would take me past Palenque through smoky jungle mountains into Zapatista-held territory, where the Mexican army and the rebels stared uneasily at each other across barricades—and finally on to San Cristóbal de Las Casas, which I'd entered the previous October from the Pacific side by way of Juchitán.

In a half hour I arrived, brakes screeching, at the outskirts of Palenque Town.

I found the Hotel Xibalbá on a tree-shaded, pothole-pitted lane—a two-story stucco building set among banana palms and banyans, its restaurant and reception desk open to the street.

It seemed a strange name for a hotel: Xibalbá. In ancient Mayan cosmology, the universe was composed of three realms—celestial, earthly, and lower. Each had numerous subdivisions—the underworld having, like Dante's hell, nine. I knew *Xibalbá* meant "underworld." Hotel Underworld. Was this macabre Mayan wit at play?

At the reception desk I asked if David Lebrun and crew were here. They're out shooting, said the petite bespectacled clerk. They usually come back after sunset.

Relieved at the news, glad to have reached journey's end for the day, I followed a small dark man bearing my luggage down the street, past a house with a front yard full of barking Dobermans, to the Hotel Xibalbá's other wing—a small building modeled after the A-frame corbel vault used in Mayan temple construction. He led me into a simple, clean second-floor room with air conditioning—less a convenience than a necessity, as temperatures climbed to 120 degrees here in midsummer. A faded "Mesa Redonda" poster hung over the bed, celebrating the roundtable conferences begun in Palenque in 1973 devoted to the decipherment of Mayan script. Another above the dresser portrayed a dramatically lit photo of the head of Pakal, the great ruler and builder of Palenque in its seventh-century heyday. On the little television's lone station, a Mayan woman wearing a huipil was reading the news in what sounded like Tzotzil, a dialect spoken around San Cristóbal.

Opening the curtain, I saw that I faced directly down upon the front yard of the house separating the two wings of the hotel. The fidgety Dobermans, seeing me, unleashed a series of despondent moans.

Palenque Town, as Santo Domingo de Palenque is better known, was a low-slung scramble of tacky shops and hostels that existed mainly to serve visitors to the ruins. Fifty years ago Palenque was known mainly to archaeologists and adventurers; now it was a hot stop on the Mundo Maya route. Mestizo Mexicans, ethnic Mayans, and foreign backpackers in T-shirts, shorts, and sandals idled along the rutted streets in the dying day. Indigenous women from the highlands, dressed in colorful huipiles and indigo skirts, folded woven scarves resting on their heads, lent a noble, harmonious counterpoint.

I drove down Calle Juárez, the main drag, casting about for an e-mail place, the silver Tstratus providing amusement along the sidewalks each time I braked. It wasn't uncommon in Mexican towns and cities to find three Internet cafés on a single block, and they were cheap—as little as a dollar an hour. Paradoxically, the poorer the town or country, the more Internet cafés there were, as people without the means to log on at home did it in public. Spotting one by the bus station, I pulled over and took my place among a klatch of young backpackers. The colored screen bloomed before me, compressed to the size of the monitor, and suddenly there was the world as headlines: Bush's bluster, Putin's Chechen woes, JLo's latest peccadilloes, Osama's bearded mug. I checked my messages, answered a few, then walked back out into the pulsing heat of the darkening town. At a tienda next door I bought a few things for the room, then drove back to the Xibalbá.

Waiting for David in the hotel restaurant, I sipped a tequila, stealing glances at the only other people in sight— a beautiful young European couple at dinner, mooning over each other, whispering endearments in a Slavic tongue. Polish? Czech? Hungarian? He was tall, lean, and tan, with a strong, delicate face and large eyes; she, his female match, had willowy bare arms, tumbling hair, full lips, and flaring cheekbones. They couldn't stop looking at each other, reaching across the table to caress the gold bands on each other's fingers. Wrenching my gaze away, I began studying a large aerial-survey detail map hung on the wall beside me. It showed, in red, the fifteen or so of Palenque's ruins excavated so far, and hundreds of gray sites located but still marked "unexplored"—more than six hundred in all.

Nobody knows how many Mayan villages, towns, and cities lie undiscovered throughout the forests and jungles of four countries. *Chicleros*, the men who search for the *chicle* tree to satisfy the world's taste for chewing gum, hacking through the southern lowlands of present-day Guatemala and southern Mexico, keep coming upon the remnants of previously unknown Mayan centers. By the first century A.D. at least twenty-five distinct Mayan city-states had been built out of rock, limestone, and lime mortar, all without the use of metal or wheels. Among the grandest—Copan in Honduras, Tikal in Guatemala, Chichén Itzá and Cobá in the Yucatán—Palenque had always held special prominence among investigators.

David's two-month itinerary had offered a range of intriguing choices. After Palenque and some weeks around the Yucatán, they were to fly to Guatemala to film an ancient Mayan festival in the village of Rabanal, and from there to vast Copan. But the chance to join them at Palenque had been too good to pass up. The tales of intrepid adventurers, the evocative early illustrations, the black and white photos of grizzled explorers standing before great shards and fragments of inscriptions and overgrown temples—the sheer romance of the place—had beguiled me.

If Mayan studies generally tended to attract obsessives and adventurers who flirted with reason's edge—conspiratorial

Atlanteans, religious fanatics, compulsive dreamers, wrong-headed linguists—no site had drawn more of them than Palenque. Since the arrival of the Spaniards, the ancient city had taken the measure of those who approached its riddles, driving some to the brink of madness, rewarding others with momentous finds—the unearthing of great tombs, the decoding of texts—discoveries that continued today.

The names bear mythic resonance to the initiates: Antonio del Río and his artist, Alamendárez, among the first Europeans to arrive, in 1787; the Anglo-Irish explorer Juan Galindo, who reached Palenque in 1831; the bizarre French artist Count Jean Frédéric Waldeck, who already well into his sixties slept among the ruins for fourteen months. The self-proclaimed linguist Constantine Samuel Rafinesque-Smaltz was the first to recognize that Palenque's stone inscriptions and the brush-painted texts found in the so-called Dresden Codex were written in the same script. There was the formidable American explorer James Lloyd Stephens and his English artist companion Frederick Catherwood, whose 1840 Palenque drawings still haunt the imagination. In 1922 the Danish archaeologist Franz Blom came within steps of discovering Pakal's tomb—possibly the most spectacular pre-Hispanic find ever—a prize that fell instead to the Spanish-Mexican archaeologist Alberto Ruz Lhuillier in 1954.

"Its architecture sings out to us with a Mozartian sort of richness and classical elegance," one rapturous commentator wrote of Palenque. Here in the rainy jungle foothills of the Sierra Oriental de Chiapas, where five tributaries of the great

Usumacinta River converge, the people who built this city inscribed their rulers' history in stone glyphs—those peculiar blocks that sometimes look like complex cartoons—that lay unseen and unread for centuries, then were wrongly read for several more. It was the dramatic story of their ultimate decipherment that David had come to make a film about.

I heard the sound of wheels on gravel. Looking up, I saw David and his crew piling out of a minivan in front of the Hotel Xibalbá. They looked tired, dirty, and happy.

"You made it!" David called.

Hugs, laughter, grins. These were old friends from California. I'd known David for years, his wife Amy, and Rosey, the producer on this film, a long time as well.

David was beaming. "We're getting incredible stuff. We've had total access to the temples for the last five days."

"Except Amy fell down the palace temple stairs today and almost got herself killed," Rosey said. "Fortunately she did a tuck and roll and stopped herself at the first platform."

I looked at Amy, alarmed.

"Just a little sore in the shoulders," she said. "I could use a good massage. Join us for dinner?" She continued unloading equipment, exhibiting a nonchalance she might or might not be feeling. Amy was a camera and lighting professional and, clearly, a trouper.

A huge white Panavision Mexico equipment truck rumbled past and parked in front of the building where I was staying. Two young Mexican guys and a gringo jumped down and joined us.

"Raúl. Xavier. Our drivers, grips, and electricians," said David.

"*Mucho gusto.*"

Rosey introduced me to Steve, the other cameraman.

"Quick showers, then we'll be down," David said. "We're going to a restaurant back by the ruins."

As we began to gather, one by one, for dinner, I thought about Amy's near-fall. Eerily, two months earlier other friends had e-mailed from Palenque saying they'd watched a man tumble to his death that morning from the top stairs of the Temple of the Inscriptions, across from the palace Amy had fallen from. The man had landed on the ground at their feet. It had utterly traumatized them and haunted their dreams still.

"So have you met the Dobermans yet?" Rosey asked.

"They're hard to miss," I said.

"They're driving me nuts," Steve the cameraman said, swilling a beer. "They go all night. You'll see."

Maybe they're the guardians of Xibalbá, the underworld, I thought but didn't say aloud.

We piled into the minivan, minus Steve, who had some calls to make, and Raúl and Javier, who were off to meet Raúl's new love interest, a local Palenque girl. As Rosey drove us in the direction of the ruins, David told me a little about Steve, an experienced nature cameraman who'd lived in Morocco for two years shooting in the Sahara for PBS, another year in Belize. He also led nature safaris in Kenya. For all that, David said, the

Dobermans were bedeviling him, and he hadn't slept the last two nights.

"I think Steve's about ready to slit their throats," Amy said.

This team had been on the road together two weeks, with a month and a half to go. Location filming is arduous, the days long and full of variables, from weather to permits to physical obstacles. Things don't always go well; little dramas erupt. To a film crew on the road, the arrival of somebody from outside is both welcome and an intrusion, equal parts refreshment and distraction. There is a visitor's protocol, but it isn't always so easy to discern what it is. But this seemed to be a cheery enough band, buoyed by its professionalism and the fact that they seemed to be getting what they'd come for.

A few minutes beyond Palenque town, we took a turnoff marked RUINAS. Then just before the guard gate to ancient Palenque, Rosey wheeled left onto a narrow, muddy jungle path and parked beneath a tree. We clambered out into the dark and crossed a small, swaying bridge over a river deep in jungle. Suddenly we were standing in a half-lit, *palapa*-covered restaurant filled with young Mexican and international travelers in shorts and tank tops, hunkered at tables, hanging by the bar. Reggae blared from a sound system. Midriff-baring waitresses swept by carrying pizzas, burgers, and cervezas.

"Welcome to El Panchán," David said, smiling. " 'Paradise,' in Mayan."

A hip-looking waiter in dreadlocks guided us to the last available table. We ordered a couple of bottles of Chilean red wine and a local beer, Montejo (named after the Spanish conqueror of Yucatán—of all people). It felt good to be among friends after the solitary day of travel, the skittish drive from Villahermosa; yet the trendy crowd, Santana and Bob Marley and Lenny Kravitz blasting out into the Palenque jungle, drowning out the howler monkeys and whatever old ghosts might lurk about the edges of the ruins, felt odd somehow. Staring at the laminated menu, I thought of those khaki-garbed explorers and adventurers in pith helmets in the vintage photos, standing before liana-choked ruins and great broken tablets. What would old Franz Blom think if he were to awaken to find himself at this international-style eatery called Paradise, among the cool, tan youth who'd come to the great Mayan site for the *good energy, man?*

After we'd ordered food, Amy and Rosey adjourned to the tie-dye boutique by the entrance. A band mounted the stage— two gringo guitarists, a Peruvian flute player, and a congo player. David and I steeled ourselves for the worst, but their covers of Buena Vista Social Club hits and son jarocho favorites like "La Bamba," muted by our distance from the stage, actually sounded great.

"So you're happy with what you're getting," I said to David.

"We've been shooting the reliefs decorating the interior platform walls of the Temple of the Inscriptions, and other key sites—the palace, Temple of the Cross. When we first tried lighting the glyphs, it looked like we were going to have a big problem. They were too worn, not raised enough. But we figured out a way to highlight them by raking them with light from the edge, making them appear sharply delineated—as if by magic. I can tweak them later in PhotoShop. Should turn out great."

I had to smile. David had been making films since he was young, part of a generation of independent American filmmakers who bloomed in the 1960s, with roots stretching back to the experimental films of Maya Deren. Often they worked with the slimmest of means. David's earlier films, usually shot in sixteen millimeter, edited by hand, laboriously crafted on optical printers, had taken him years to complete. He'd wanted to make this film for close to a decade; now with serious funding from the National Endowment for the Humanities and the National Science Foundation, it was becoming a reality. He had a proper budget, a big truck full of fancy equipment, digital cameras, a crew, and computers waiting at the editing stage.

"I'd love to go up there with you tomorrow," I said.

"Actually we're done shooting there, except for the museum. Tomorrow we drive to Toniná, up in the highlands, to shoot the ruins."

"The city that conquered Palenque," I said. I was disappointed. I'd wanted to spend time with them at the Temple of the Inscriptions, but I'd arrived a day too late.

"Toniná's incredibly beautiful," David said. "You should come. When we traveled through here a few years ago scouting for the film, it was the one place Amy and I said, 'We could live here.' The day after tomorrow we'll shoot back here at the Palenque Museum. Possibly a bit more of the ruins."

Food arrived. Rosey and Amy rejoined us. Over the music David said, "See that guy over there?"

Several tables away a small, neatly dressed man with dark skin and close-cropped silver hair sat with a beautiful young woman, a large dog at their feet.

"That's Moisés Morales," David said. "Amazing guy. Somewhere in his eighties now. He's kind of the éminence grise around here. Fluent in four or five languages. He started out as a guide at Palenque. A lot of the Mesa Redondas have happened at his place. These days he's semiretired—attends epistemology conferences in Poland, stuff like that. And he owns a lot of real estate around town. He, or maybe it's one of his sons, owns this restaurant."

After dinner, while David and Amy visited Moisés Morales at his table, Rosey and I lingered near the bar, watching the band.

"Actually," I said, "I think that skinny bongo player is keeping the whole thing together."

"I was thinking the same thing."

"Is he a little bit cute?"

"Maybe a little." She shrugged and grinned. "But not enough."

Rosey's boyfriend was a drummer, and she was missing him a little, hoping he'd join them later in the shoot.

Driving back in the van, David asked if I was coming with them to Toniná. The ride would take them up into the Chiapas Mountains, past Ocosingo, halfway to San Cristóbal. The trip, however beautiful the setting, looked to be something of a "forced march," in Rosey's words. I wanted to spend time with them on site, and the shoot at the museum two days hence sounded decidedly less dramatic. But I'd just arrived and hadn't yet seen Palenque.

"I think I'll stay here tomorrow," I said. "Sniff your footprints while they're still warm. Are the ruins overrun with hordes?"

"Not if you get up there early, before the tours. Or late in the day when they've left."

We pulled up to the Hotel Xibalbá. I wished them good luck in Toniná.

"And you enjoy Palenque," Rosey said.

"Bring water," David said. "Wear a hat. And lean *in* when you climb the pyramid steps."

He glanced at Amy. She was rubbing her sore shoulder, gazing distantly out into the darkness, looking for the first time like someone who only a few hours earlier had glimpsed the shadow realms of Xibalbá.

15.

Conversations with Pakal

The next morning, after a night of highway dreams punctuated by keening dogs, I drove back up the Palenque road in cool air. Threads of mist twined along the Chiapan hills. Mayan farmers leveled fields of grass with machetes. I was entirely ready for a jaguar to cross my path—as had actually happened to David and Amy on an earlier trip through this region. After paying ten pesos at the guard gate, I wound up into thickening jungle. At a shaded turnaround already filling with cars and minivans, I tipped a boy to watch my car, bought a ticket, and worked my way past guides and trinket sellers to the turnstile entry.

Ruins entered through a turnstile didn't bode well. INAH, as Mexico's national cultural preservation agency is known, hadn't always shown the best judgment in these things. I thought of my recent visit to Chichén Itzá. Had Palenque been turned into a theme park? Recalling the map on the wall of the

Hotel Xibalbá restaurant, I knew this was but a small part of ancient Palenque, but it was the city center. In the guest log I was asked to sign, I noticed that almost all the non-Mexican visitors were from European countries, the Mayan regions their province especially in the winter months.

Wide stone steps led up through trees. Suddenly three large stone structures came into view, set beside each other against a hillside of dense forest, overwhelming any human presence.

The smallest one, the Temple of the Skull, had been mostly destroyed, though hundreds of jade pieces had been found in its various substructures, I'd read. The Temple of the Red Queen beside it had been the site of a rich 1993 discovery: a sarcophagus containing the remains of a royal woman, along with jewelry, various implements, a jade mask of two hundred pieces, and the bones of another woman apparently sacrificed with her. Stairs led me to the stone chamber where her tomb had been found, though it had been removed to a museum.

The largest of the three, the Temple of the Inscriptions, was intact. Pyramidal, with steps leading up the center, it divided into eight platforms as it rose some seventy feet, framed against steep forest. At its summit was a roofed, six-columned, pale limestone pavilion. Mayan structures often appear forbidding, cold—stony geometric monoliths. It doesn't help that the red paint once covering them is missing, nor that we know a fair amount about bloody Mayan rites. But the Temple of the Inscriptions breathed harmony, proportion, confidence—and mystery. I thought it was the most beautiful structure I'd ever seen.

The inscriptions tell us that A.D. 572 marked the ascent of the first king of Palenque, K'uk' B'ahlam I, or Quetzal Jaguar. After a succession of rulers the one known as Pakal, or Shield, became king at the age of twelve. During his sixty-eight-year reign, he oversaw much of Palenque's golden age, building this supreme temple and many others. Then in 711 the rival city of Toniná invaded the city, capturing Pakal's second son, in effect ending Palenque's brief, glorious era. Decline followed, and by around 900 Palenque was abandoned—as were all Mayan cities during that epoch, for reasons still debated.

From the temple's base I gazed up the sixty-nine steep stairs down which that unfortunate man had tumbled a few months earlier to his death. ("Lean *in* when you climb the pyramid steps," David had counseled.) Inside the upper pavilion, three paneled murals bore inscriptions narrating the city's history, its rulers, its divine origins—the 617 glyphs David and crew had been shooting.

On the grassy sward in front of the temple, a large marble crypt bore the remains of the archaeologist Alberto Ruz Lhuillier, who in 1952 unearthed the jewel-laden tomb of the great king Pakal. Luz discovered a secret stone stairway—the one Franz Blom had just missed—leading from the floor of the platform of inscriptions down inside the pyramid to a chamber at its base. There he found, surrounded by murals depicting the nine lords of Xibalbá, an inscribed sarcophagus containing the jewel-encrusted remains of King Pakal, along with a jade mosaic death mask and an array of jewelry and objects.

The entire temple had been constructed, as were those of ancient Egypt, to house the dead king's tomb, to connect Pakal to the province of the dead. To the Maya, to die was "entering the road." The Temple of the Inscriptions was a conduit to the afterlife, the underworld, the realm of Xibalbá.

Palenque faced out across a wide green forest plain that ran all the way to the northern tip of the Yucatán. Across the leveled center of ancient Palenque, more structures rose in the distance. I continued on to the complex known as the Palace—a vast, unrestored warren of arches, niches, platforms, courtyards, and murals built over successive generations, and where Palenque's rulers apparently lived. The Palace's tower was built, it is thought, to provide a viewing station from which to watch the sun strike the Temple of the Inscriptions during the winter solstice.

That morning, wandering the parklike agora of central Palenque, climbing among excavated ruins, I passed quiet Mayan artisans sitting on the grass before painted reproductions and statues for sale. Tours came and went, interrupting the silence with polyglot commentary. From the highest platform of the Temple of the Cross, I was able to see the tips of smaller structures not yet named but only numbered, jutting above the forest canopy, and the green plain extending below. Great finds were still being made here: recently an interior tomb similar to Pakal's had been located by radar and digital imaging in a ruin called simply Edificio XX.

Whichever clearing I came to, whichever temple stairs I mounted, my gaze inevitably drifted back to the Temple of the Inscriptions, with its shining, alabaster, sun-washed upper platform, covered with inscriptions awaiting revelation in David's film. Perfect, pristine, stone-solid yet not of this world, built to mediate between upper and lower realms, it was Palenque's true magnetic center—what had obsessed old Count Waldeck, the explorers, the linguists, the anthropologists.

When the midday heat turned fierce, I left the ruins and drove back to town. It felt strange to be walking the sweltering streets among people looking like the figures on the murals, hearing Mayan mixed with Spanish. Chol, a linguistic descendant of Cholan, the inscribed text of the great Mayan cities, is still spoken on the streets of Palenque Town.

I'd planned to continue on with David and crew to Xpujil, their next location, a six-hour drive from Palenque, then from there to some remote shooting sites. But I was worried about my rented car, the wretched Tstratus. I could drive back to Villahermosa, though it was in the opposite direction from Xpujil, and exchange it. But for what? Would the half-day or more I'd lose be worth it? If my visit was to be only these days in Palenque, I already knew I'd be content. I called Aeromexico and checked alternative return flights from Villahermosa, then drove back up to the ruins.

Entering by way of a lower gate this time, I followed a shady forest path up along a stream called Otolum. Fragments of structures peeked through fronds and tree trunks. There were few people in this area, known as the Grupo de los Murciélagos, the Bat Group. Crossing the Puente Murciélagos to a ruin on the other side of the stream, I thought how these Spanish terms were just guesses. The ancient residents didn't speak of their city as Palenque; they may have called it Lakam Ha (Big Water), referring either to this river or to the plateau above, which floods in the rainy season, giving it the appearance of a lake. If most of the inscriptions' meanings have been puzzled out, only recently have linguists managed to determine how many of the words were spoken—figuring back from contemporary Chol, or Yucatecan, or one of the thirty distinct dialects contemporary Mayas speak. Whatever they called Palenque, and however they said it, this cool, damp canyon of palms and banyans and mossy rocks must have been where people came on hot afternoons to escape the heat, rest, swim in the pools beneath the feathery waterfalls, and fall in love.

I paused at a spot on a rock alone by one of the falls. Scraps of light played on leaves and water. A flock of wild parrots screeched somewhere above. I peeled a mango I'd bought in town and began to eat it. How paradisical, I thought, juice dripping down my fingers. Panchán indeed. Here lived Gaugin's nineteenth-century Tahitian dream and so much more—the vast and variegated landscapes, the rich romance of lost civilizations, the majestic haunted ruins. In this deep forest, more than in the manicured clearing above where the main excavations lay, lurked the primeval vision of twisting, overgrown liana and fractured stones Frederick Catherwood had drawn 165 years ago.

Yet Palenque, for all its idyllic beauty, must have been a

terrifying civilization to live in: human sacrifice, bloodletting, penis-piercing, ballgames to the death. Until the recent work of linguists like Knorosov allowed us to read their texts, generations of scholars had imagined these great builders, writers, and calendar makers to be more concerned with poetry and metaphysics—not the litany of kings, dynasties, and warfare the decipherments have revealed.

A stillness had settled upon the afternoon. It was tempting to just strip and drop into the beautiful pool at the base of the falls. There seemed to be nobody else around. I started to take off my shirt when I noticed two khaki-clad figures above me, leaning against a rock, deep in a kiss. When they drew apart, I saw it was the beautiful couple I'd seen at dinner at the Hotel Xibalbá.

I worked my way slowly upstream, lingering in the cool *sombra*. By the time I reached the plateau of the upper excavations, it was late afternoon. Sun tipped the rim of Sierra de Chiapas above the Temple of the Inscriptions. Few visitors remained on the grounds. When I turned to climb back down the canyon to my car, I found the path to the lower exit closed off. Recrossing the site, I left the way I'd first come in that morning, by way of the main entrance, then walked down the jungle road in the fading light to my car.

Back at the Hotel Xibalbá, I saw the crew's van and equipment truck parked outside. Steve the cameraman was at the reception desk. They'd had a good day's shooting at Toniná, he said, in spite of the long drive. Then he asked me, somewhat sheepishly, if I'd help him fill something out in Spanish.

It was a complaint form, addressed to the local tourist board.

"I almost got thrown in jail last night," Steve said.

It turned out that while we'd been at dinner at El Panchán, Steve had had a run-in with the Dobermans' owner outside the front yard. With a few beers under his belt, he'd made an impolite comment about the dogs, a shouting match had ensued, and the man had called the police. Only the intercession of a local guide had saved Steve from jail.

I was helping Steve write up his complaint when David arrived. He wasn't so convinced this was a good idea. Apparently the house next door belonged to Merle Greene Robertson, a venerable North American Maya hand. "She's in the States right now," David said. "The guy staying there is the brother of a colleague of hers. The dogs are his." They were all part of the local hierarchy of Mayanists, he said, including venerable Moíses Morales, that had blessed the making of the film.

Merle Greene, whom I'd read of in Michael Coe's *Breaking the Maya Code*, had lived in Palenque for decades, her illustrations and photographs and stone rubbings contributing much to recent decipherment breakthroughs. Her house, David said, had been the site of the first Mesa Redonda, the annual conference that had nurtured so many recent breakthroughs in Mayan epigraphy, as the study of ancient writing systems is known.

"But we want people to file these grievances," the hotel receptionist said. "We're losing clients. Only this morning a woman planning to stay here a week left after one night because of those dogs. If there are enough complaints, the police will issue a *demanda* on the owner. Then he'll have to do something."

Steve decided, as a compromise, to file the complaint—but on the way out of town, after shooting was completed.

With this issue behind us, we all settled down to dinner at the Xibalbá restaurant, David, Amy, and Rosey enthusing about the day at Toniná—the inscriptions, the beauty of the setting, even the roadblocks on the drive up and back as they passed through regions controlled alternately by rebel Zapatistas on one side of the road and the Mexican army on the other. Still, I couldn't imagine a richer day than the one I'd had at Palenque.

The next morning, bearing coffee for the crew, I arrived at the Palenque Museum, across from the lower entry to the ruins. Inside, where they'd already begun setting up their first shot, a contretemps with the museum director was in progress. He wanted to charge them extra for the use of their electricity. The mood was dark; David wasn't inclined to bow to this small extortion. It looked like they might have to run the day's shoot off their own generator in the big truck parked outside.

The low, airy new museum housed some of the best pieces from recent site excavations. Steve was setting up a shot before one of them, a tall panel from a structure known as Edificio XVII. Amy, on a ladder, was engaged in the subtle task of lighting the raised stone images, using a variety of nets and scrims. Raúl and Xavier were hauling things in from the truck outside, moving wires and cables about.

David's script, a two-hour adaptation of *Breaking the Maya Code*, bore all the human intrigue and scholarly sleuthing of an A. S. Byatt novel. Composed of moving images, still images, and animation sequences, it would include live interviews with the most important contemporary Mayanists who had figured in the breakthroughs. But the visual core of the work, and the trickiest part, were these location shots, moving and stationary, of the panels and inscriptions from the great temples. To this end, they'd brought with them this army of equipment, including seven cameras, digital and nondigital, of varying sizes.

The panel they were preparing to shoot depicted a captive king, Chan Bahlum II, in A.D. 695, kneeling at the feet of his subjugator, who wore a large headdress with the image of the war serpent and held a spear and a flexible shield. Twenty-one glyphs recounted the occasion. The twelve-foot-high stone image, spectacularly vivid under Amy's lighting, retained traces of "Maya blue," that mysterious tint impervious to chemical explanation that doesn't fade, and the red dye composed of rust often used in Mayan interior and exterior art.

Negotiations with the museum director about the electricity had broken down. "Damn," Rosey said irritably. "This sort of thing has been going on the whole trip." The little extra charges, over and above what had originally been negotiated, were carving thousands of unexpected dollars out of their budget.

Hearing the generator start up, I walked outside to the big Panavision truck. Luis and Xavier's domain, it was crammed with dollies and cameras, screens and baffles, ladders and cords and boxes and lights.

While setups continued inside the museum, I looked at one of the next panels they'd be shooting, found during the 1993 excavation of Edificio XIX. A horizontal frieze of extreme drama and beauty, it described a creation-myth sequence David thought he might use to open his film.

Throughout the morning I played gofer, watched the crew shoot the astonishing panels, and did a little translating for Amy and Rosey. After lunch, as filming slowed into its arc of technical repetition, I slipped away, irresistibly drawn back to the site for a final visit. I wanted to climb to those more hidden structures where the tablets they were shooting in the museum had been found.

The path led up into dark, thick-treed jungle mountainside. The air cooled; the sounds from the site below died away. There seemed to be nobody else in this part of Palenque. Passing a small ruin on my right identified on the map as Edificio XXI, I came to the larger Edificio XIX, shrouded in heavy forest.

Carefully leaning in, grabbing old vine roots for support, I climbed broken stairs slippery with wet leaves and moss. At the top, in the deep shadow of a roofed stone pavilion, I came to the reproduction David had told me I'd find: the panel with its creation myth text, whose original they'd been shooting at the museum when I'd left.

Standing in the dim, empty, half-ruined edifice, enveloped by jungle, I noticed how light barely penetrated these temples, even in midday. The murals and inscriptions, so brightly lit in the museum, would have lain in darkness most of the time—fully visible, even to the Maya who created them, only by firelight or torchlight. Maybe that was part of their magical power—little different, in that sense, from a movie theater today. Like the early Maya, we wait in the dark, expectant; then illumination spreads, the story is revealed.

For a flickering moment, at the top of Edificio XIX, I thought I'd glimpsed the heart of the film David was making.

That night we all drove back to El Panchán for a farewell dinner, Steve and Xavier and Raúl joining us this time. Parking on the jungle road, we crossed the bridge to find El Panchán in full swing again, another full complement of young travelers disporting themselves among the palapas. Live Andean music filled the air this night—flutes, guitars, a soft thumping drum. Moíses Morales was holding court at the head of a long table.

We found our way to a spot near the back. The mood among us was festive. From here the crew was leaving early the next day for tiny Xpujil, on the long road east to Chetumal. Xpujil was well off the tourist route—no El Panchán there, few Euro-hippies—but within an hour's drive of the huge ancient

Mayan city of Calakmul, only recently excavated in parts, and Chicanná, another site David wanted to shoot. From there they'd continue up and across the Mayan Yucatán—Playa del Carmen, Izamal, Maní, Mérida—before flying on to Guatemala. I hated to miss Xpujil, but with ever less faith that the Tstratus would get me there, let alone back, I'd booked a flight back to Mexico City leaving the next morning. So tonight it was *saluds*, glasses raised to Palenque, the film, *toda la vida*.

"Set your alarms for an early start tomorrow," David said to his crew.

"The dogs will take care of that," Steve said with a dark laugh.

When we got back to the Xibalbá, the guardians to the underworld were already appealing in chorus to an unseen moon. I went to the reception counter to settle my bill, as I'd be leaving at the crack of dawn the next day. The beautiful couple I'd seen at dinner my first night here, then by the waterfall at Palenque, were there, dressed in tank tops and shorts and sandals, their arms around each other's waists, backpacks leaning up against the wall. They were checking out too—taking a night bus to San Cristóbal, I guessed, or maybe across the Yucatán to some beach south of Cancún to swim in the warm Caribbean, eat fresh ceviche, make love in a hammock.

Down through the years, as children came, mundane life settled upon them in Prague (Warsaw? Budapest?), and gray streaked their hair, what of Palenque would remain with them? The dreamy candlelit dinners? The kisses under the falls? Perhaps in the end something not that different from what I'd take away: the indelible afterimage of the Temple of the Inscriptions, a beauty remote yet present; jungle ruins, bearing traces of things unvoiced and unseen that lurk in the substrata of dreams; mysteries of origins—and glimpses of Panchán, paradise.

16.

Fridamania

That afternoon, back in Mexico City, I checked into the Hotel Milan, planning to catch an early bus the next day for the five-hour trip back to Xalapa. I was ready for coffee and orchids, the little yellow house in the fog. And it was time to finish the magazine article, the ostensible engine of my Mexico travels.

In *la capital* the first wave of Fridamania had already hit, though the film wasn't yet in release. Sumptuous, homegrown Salma Hayek, producing and starring in *Frida* as the star-crossed Mexican artist and feminist icon, had given a round of interviews the day before to the Mexican press—even tossing in a couple of references to her role in *Once Upon a Time in Mexico*, "recently concluded shooting in San Miguel de Allende." In one interview, Salma referred to Frida's gargantuan painter husband Diego Rivera as a *cogelón*—a term I understood to mean "fucker," though whether in the sense of being a "shit" or a guy who likes to screw a lot, I didn't know. I was sure my film critic friend Eduardo would enlighten me.

It was a quiet late Saturday afternoon in the capital, the traffic easing, the February cool, even faintly fresh. A taxi took me from the Milan to the wide, pretty plaza of Coyoacán, the suburban neighborhood where Frida and Diego had lived. At one remove from the capital, Coyoacán had been a separate village, and the reigning midcentury artists' retreat, until the advancing city had swallowed it.

I found Eduardo at a café on the plaza, sipping a *cortado*—an espresso with a dollop of milk—having just come from a press junket at Frida's famous blue house a few blocks away.

"Well, Diego *was* a cogelón," he said. "A guy who liked to sleep with lots of different women. We're not so prudish as you gringos, but it's not an expression a beautiful Mexican *actriz* like Salma is supposed to use in interviews. So that helps stir up a little controversy for the movie, right?"

In Mexican slang, taking the name of something and adding -*ón* gives emphasis, often negative. *Cabrón. Chingón. Coger* in Mexico is a favored verb for "fuck," along with *joder*, though in Spain *coger* is used only in its literal meaning of "to grab." So while you might say to your friend in Madrid, "Let's *coger* a taxi," this would suggest to a Mexican a ridiculous, not to mention impossible, act. Here in Mexico City you'd better *aggarar* that taxi, or *tomar* it, but don't *coger* it.

"You'd never hear María Félix or Dolores Del Río in their day say *cogelón* in public." Eduardo took out his tobacco pouch, spilling grains on the table. "But then, Salma doesn't fit the mold. Her father's family is Lebanese. Frida Kahlo's father was a German Jew. So they're what you guys would call hyphenated Mexicans. Of course almost every Mexican is a hyphen. When the British conquered North America, they killed off the Indians; here, our conquistadores slept with them. Hence the mestizo. But it's not just Spanish and Indian blood. The truth is we're as mixed up racially as you in the States."

This face of Mexico had revealed itself to me slowly. The graduated scale from pure Indian to pure Spanish was everywhere in evidence. But there was more to the story, a montage of origins inviting a much richer perception of Mexico. Countless Africans brought here to work the plantations along the Caribbean coast had blended over the centuries into the population; some still lived in black farming and fishing communities along both southern coasts, descendants of ex-slaves who had escaped their masters. French settlers arrived during the time of Maximilian and stayed on, as did German, English, and U.S. miners and engineers in the Bajio region, where I lived. Irish soldiers who'd fought alongside Mexicans in the revolution settled here, St. Patrick's Day now firmly installed on the Mexican calendar and celebrated every year with parades. Japanese-Mexicans, Chinese-Mexicans, Filipino-Mexicans traced roots dating back more than a century—the same period when Middle Eastern and Jewish settlers from the Levant and Europe began arriving, among them Frida's father Guillermo Kahlo, a fine photographer of colonial architecture. Émigrés from all over Central and South America had found, and still did, safe haven in Mexico.

"So I saw a rough cut of the film," Eduardo said. "Pure melodrama. But then, so were Frida and Diego's lives. What should we expect? And I mean, *fíjate*, Geoffrey Rush as Trotsky? I'm sorry."

The Russian political exile, one of Frida's many lovers, had been brutally assassinated in his house not far from where we sat. I could see *Frida* wasn't going to get an easy ride in Eduardo's weekly column.

"I'll tell you this, though," he said. "Both Frida and Salma have great breasts."

Eduardo, otherwise cosmopolitan and sensitive and smart, considered his unreconstructed, unapologetic Mexican machismo as simply healthy male erotic appetite.

"The Che Guevara film will be worse, I promise you. A Latino *On the Road*." He fished in his jacket for coffee change. "Did you know Che tried to find work as an actor when he arrived in Mexico in 'fifty-four? Just before he joined up with Fidel. A greater role awaited him, no?"

We parted with an abrazo. I walked on alone to Frida's house, thinking how days and nights of curating fantasies in dark screening rooms inevitably turn passionate young film buffs—I'd known so many in L.A.—into cynics.

I came to the high walls of Frida's corner house, freshly painted its trademark *azul añil*, a deep saturated pre-Hispanic blue used to ward off evil spirits. The old rambling house where the artist had grown up, and where she and Diego later lived, had lately been remodeled to more resemble a museum, its new gift shop crammed with Frida memorabilia. Seeing a crowd of foreign tourists emerge laden with purchases, I recalled Xavier's comment that day in San Miguel: *If I see another Frida Kahlo tote bag, I'm getting out my gun.*

The cult seemed unstoppable. Amazon's site listed eighty-three books under Frida's name; a Lycos web search yielded 106,040 entries. Living in the artistic and physical shadow of the gargantuan Diego during her lifetime, the besieged painter with the run-on eyebrows, who died in 1953, had now surpassed her husband as icon if not artist. The phenomenon had begun sometime in the 1970s, then picked up speed with the publication of Hayden Herrera's 1991 biography. Now Frida's somber, serially repetitive visage decorates refrigerator magnets, stationery, pens, and posters to the ends of the earth.

Still, the poignancy of arriving at her bed, overhung by a mirror so she could paint lying down until the end, struck hard. *The Broken Column*: in the collision of a bus with a tram when she was eighteen, an iron rod had skewered her left hip, emerging through her vagina, leaving her with a permanently damaged spinal column, in pain for the rest of her life.

The interior and gardens still housed some of the Mexican *artesanías* Frida and Diego had collected with a passion—little pre-Hispanic clay figurines, ingenious wooden games and toys, giant papier-mâché *calaveras*, skeletons—part of a midcentury revival of nativist *mexicanismo* they'd championed. I'd found this same fertile invention intact in the markets of Guanajuato, on the streets of San Cristóbal, in the villages of Oaxaca, in spite of every modern pressure to abandon it.

Few of Frida's original works hung in the house, save some

early portraits of others. Most of her better-known paintings rested in the hands of Dolores Olmedo, an earlier wife of Diego's and now *patrona* of her own private museum in the city. Frida's canvases, seen live, were smaller than one would have guessed from their packed drama, just as she who loomed so vividly in her own art was dwarfed physically by her elephantine husband. A strange, almost unpleasant morbidity attached itself to her work and her circumstance, and the paintings show little technical range. Yet the fecund imaginings, the relentless self-gaze—Frida in a jungle adorned by parrots; two Fridas in hospital beds as seen from above in her abortion fantasy; Frida in man's haircut and suit—portrayed the examined life in extremis, a perfect mirror for narcissistic times. The costumes she often wore and depicted herself in—the same worn by those forceful Tehuana matriarchs of coastal Oaxaca whose extravagant textile work Masako's book would celebrate—suggested a strength Frida didn't have but had willed into herself.

Seen through a reduced postmodern lens, Frida and Diego appeared an outsize couple, living in an extravagant era filled with art and revolution. French surrealist guru André Breton, enraptured by Frida, described her as "a young woman . . . endowed with all the gifts of seduction . . . who like the shaft of light shed by the quetzal, scatters opals on the stones she passes." Faced with her husband's voracious artistic and sexual appetites, she cultivated her own, taking lovers of both genders, among them the sculptor Isamu Noguchi and the fifty-seven-year-old Trotsky. Stormy relationships, myriad liaisons, artistic genius, tragedy, infidelity, betrayal, and political intrigue: it was inevitable her story would be brought to the screen. (In fact, it already had, a decade earlier, in a Mexican film, *Las Dos Fridas*.) Now with the publication of her illustrated diaries—on sale at the gift shop on my way out—and Salma Hayek's new opus, Frida's ascension as art and feminism's Virgin of Guadalupe would be complete.

High, wispy clouds drifted past the wide windows of the Ado de Lujo bus on the long ride east to Xalapa the next day. As we rumbled across the stubbly, spreading Puebla plain, I realized this scene was as familiar to me from movies as from reality. But then Mexico had long served as cinematic backlot to the North American imagination: mysteries, romances, and Westerns; sex bombs and Latin lovers; spitfires and *cogelones*: María Félix, Dolores Del Río, Rita Hayworth, Raquel Welch, Anthony Quinn. Here in Mexico some of film's great directors had found artistic liberation.

One morning in San Miguel, soon after my first arrival there, I was on the way to the *biblioteca* to return a book when I stopped at the town's only health food store for a *licuado*. I fell into conversation with a white-bearded, ruddy-faced American named Tom Shaw—John Huston's assistant director, it turned out, there to set up locations for a film in Pozos, a nearby abandoned mining town. By then Huston was elderly and quite ill, his emphysema preventing him from making the trip up into this thin mountain air from Las Caletas, his home south of Puerto Vallarta; it would turn out to prevent him from making the film there at all. We adjourned to the jardín, where Shaw— echoing Bogie in the famous lottery ticket scene of Huston's *Treasure of the Sierra Madre*—stopped for a shoeshine. We talked for a while longer.

I knew Huston had been in and out of Mexico since the making of *The Night of the Iguana* in 1964 and that he'd shot *Under the Volcano* in Cuernavaca a few years back. In fact, the book I was returning to the library that morning was a collection of short stories by B. Traven, the author of *The Treasure of the Sierra Madre*, which Huston had filmed, unforgettably, in Mexico in 1948. But I had no idea of the extent of the director's involvement with the country, which spanned six decades and existed on many levels besides the extraordinary films he made here.

In 1925 Huston, then nineteen, arrived in postrevolutionary Veracruz on board a ship called *The American Banker*. There were buzzards in the streets, beggars everywhere, and the road to Mexico City was thick with *bandidos*. In Mexico City he befriended bullfighters, rode with Mexican horsemen, spent time in jail, accepted an honorary commission in the Mexican army, and was challenged to a gunfight. Back in California, when a woman turned down his proposal of marriage, he sailed to Acapulco by boat, then undertook a seventeen-day mule trek back to Mexico City. (Eventually he returned to L.A. and married the woman, Dorothy Harvey.) At various times he invested in a gold mine, a silver mine, and a hotel. He adopted a Mexican boy. He was friends with Mexican presidents, revolutionaries, filmmakers, bullfighters, and artists.

In 1940 Huston began a correspondence with a strange, reclusive writer living in San Cristóbal de las Casas. Eight years would pass before he'd shoot one of the world's great films, *The Treasure of the Sierra Madre*, in the mountains of Michoacán, with Humphrey Bogart, the director's father Walter—and the bizarre, secretive author, B. Traven, in attendance, incognito, as his own agent, Hal Croves. (The identity of B. Traven remained a subject of heated speculation for decades. Was he a German anarchist named Ret Marut? The illegitimate son of Kaiser Wilhelm? Hal Croves from Chicago, whom he sometimes impersonated? Meanwhile, his books and short stories became part of the Mexican school curriculum.)

Huston returned to Mexico in 1959 to shoot a western in Durango, *The Unforgiven*, with a large, expensive cast that included Burt Lancaster, Audrey Hepburn, Audie Murphy, and Lillian Gish. During delays in filming, Huston and some buddies flew in a small plane into eastern Veracruz State—the region where my bus ride was taking me—to rendezvous with temple robbers selling off priceless early Olmec artifacts. Huston smuggled some very large pieces into the States, then to his home in Ireland. In the end, *The Unforgiven* quickly sank of its own weight.

Fifteen years later Huston, Elizabeth Taylor, Richard Burton, Ava Gardner, Deborah Kerr, Sue Lyon, and much of the entire world's press descended upon the tiny coastal resort of Puerto Vallarta, where Huston was turning Tennessee Williams's play *The Night of the Iguana* into a film. The media attention and seething intrigues among the cast—in the midst of which a fall from a collapsed balcony broke Tom Shaw's back—put slumbering, steamy Puerto Vallarta on the international map.

From then on Huston wrote, worked, and disported at Las Calacas, his home south of Puerto Vallarta, among family, lovers, animals, visitors, and colleagues. In 1984 he shot what would be his last Mexico film, *Under the Volcano*, from Malcolm Lowry's novel, with Albert Finney playing the drunken, raging consul.

In the jardín that day, while Tom Shaw got his shoeshine, we started talking about the great Russian director Sergei Eisenstein's unfinished Mexico film, *¡Qué Viva México!* I hadn't known it existed until a few nights earlier, when I'd seen it on video at my friends Paul and Mina's house. Eisenstein had been invited to Hollywood to work in the late 1920s—a fiasco, as it would turn out to be for so many foreign directors: the creator of *Battleship Potemkin* couldn't possibly be contained within the American filmmaking paradigm. In 1930, taking up an invitation Diego Rivera extended when they'd met in Moscow, Eisenstein crossed into Mexico. Deeply inspired by what he found here, he began making a film on the country, with backing provided by the well-heeled brother of the muckraking U.S. journalist Upton Sinclair. Organized as a series of vignettes, the film included stunning Mayan sequences shot at Yucatán's Chichén Itzá; staged battles of the Mexican Revolution, replete with trains and bullets and hordes of costumed extras; and a wedding ceremony among the people of Tehuantepec (whose extravagant headpieces and dresses Frida/Salma would champion before the world). Before Eisenstein could complete his film, Stalin summoned him back to Moscow. To refuse would have been, literally, fatal. The footage lay unseen for decades in Moscow's film archives until Eisenstein's longtime Russian cinematographer assembled, edited, and released it, under the title *¡Qué Viva México!*

Tom Shaw was on his way to Marfil, the old bohemian suburb of Guanajuato, to have dinner with a blacklisted screenwriter friend of his and Huston's who had lived there since the 1950s. Mexico had welcomed so many exiles, emigrés, expatriates, and simply weary travelers over the years. I thought of my Haitian poet friend Arnaud, who'd waited out Papa Doc Duvalier's demise in San Miguel; and of Guatemalan novelists I'd met who, fleeing death squads, had found asylum in Mexico. John Huston was another link in that chain of artists and writers—the photographers Edward Weston and Tina Modotti, Gabriel García Márquez, Burroughs and Kerouac and Cassady—who'd found respite, succor, and inspiration here. By the time he died at Las Calacas in 1987, John Huston was a part of Mexico more than any other place.

Eastward toward the Caribe in the Ado de Lujo bus, past signs that said CERVEZA, FRENOS, GRUAS. Central Mexico was far behind us now. I touched my forehead to the cool pane, feeling lost to the day of travel behind me, ready for this Mexican bus ride to end.

Quite different from the one Luis Buñuel had shot in Mexico in 1951, in the lawless western mountains of Guerrero. *Mexican Bus Ride* (*Subida al Cielo* in Spanish), probably the Spanish director's best-loved film, follows the story of a village boy who, when his mother takes ill, boards a bus in search of a doctor. An epic adventure ensues, embroiling the boy and the other passengers in a series of riotous mishaps and revelations.

Buñuel had arrived in Mexico in 1946, joining the exodus from Spain in the wake of the Spanish Civil War and Franco's takeover. He lived and worked here for thirty-six years, eventually becoming a Mexican citizen.

As a university student in Madrid, Buñuel roomed with Federico García Lorca and Salvador Dalí, then in Paris moved quickly to the center of the surrealist movement; his scandalous *Un Chien Andalou*, made with Dalí, was the first great surrealist film. While Eisenstein was filming at Paris's Billancourt studio, Buñuel was on the next set making the shocking *L'Age d'Or*, whose erotic violations caused such an uproar it was closed down after a week and wasn't exhibited in Paris again for fifty years.

In 1930, Buñuel found himself in Hollywood, drinking around Chaplin's pool with Eisenstein, who was soon to leave for Mexico. Hollywood didn't go any better for Buñuel, and before long he returned to Europe. He was working for the Spanish Embassy in Paris when Dalí introduced him to the wealthy

British surrealist and aesthete Edward James, who, eager to support the Spanish Republican cause, offered to buy them a huge bomber.

Buñuel spent the war years in New York, hired by Nelson Rockefeller (whose family would commission, then destroy, Diego Rivera's Leninist mural at Rockefeller Center) to work at the Museum of Modern Art. Back in Hollywood at war's end, Buñuel again had little luck and headed for Mexico. Here he made dozens of films, working on twenty-four-day shooting schedules, editing in three or four days. His 1951 realist film *Los Olvidados*, about Mexico City street urchins, outraged much of Mexico but earned him a Best Director award at Cannes.

Buñuel liked to write his screenplays at San José Purua, the hotel and thermal spa in the mountains of Michoacán where John Huston and his cast and crew had stayed while making *The Treasure of the Sierra Madre*. Buñuel and Huston often used the same Mexican cinematographer, Gabriel Figueroa, whose stark, sumptuous black and white images burned Mexico into in the foreign imagination. Even after he was able to return to Europe and make *Viridiana, Belle de Jour, The Discreet Charm of the Bourgeoisie,* and *That Obscure Object of Desire,* Buñuel's home remained Mexico.

Everybody knew everybody in Mexico back then, it seemed. Buñuel and Breton. Trotsky, whom the artist Siqueiros tried to assassinate. Sergei and Huston, Diego and Frida. Edward James, who seemed to know everybody. The painter Remedios Varo and her husband, the French surrealist poet

Benjamin Péret. Raúl Hellmer, the gringo jarocho. Che and Fidel—even Lee Harvey Oswald. All interconnected, their histories overlapping. The world seemed smaller then, once upon a time in Mexico.

The rain eased, the bus flattened onto a straightaway. Clearing steam from the window with my jacket sleeve, I saw below, through the darkness, a wavering bowl of light: Xalapa, at last.

17.

Restless Fiesta

Moving through time and space, we invent fictions to propel ourselves into fact. The reasons for things often turn out to be other than they first appeared. A journey—and what isn't a journey?—picks up a narrative of its own. The map we set out with turns out to have been a figment, a fraud, a useless scrap of paper.

By the time I returned to Xalapa that night late in February 2002, San Miguel de Allende, and our house there, lay quiet again, the movie crew long departed. Masako was soon to arrive back from Oaxaca. I certainly had enough material to write a magazine article on what was interesting around Mexico today. The jolting reality of the September 11 attacks would reverberate for years, but the world wouldn't end today, it seemed. A coincident series of displacements had set me in motion. Now the fact was that I no longer knew why I was out there traveling. I was out there because I was out there.

In the grip of a pleasurable indefinition, floating in a brine of uncertainty, all notions of home, family, nation, and work had become fluid, conditional. This seemed to me an entirely appropriate state, matching reality. I felt I could carry on like this endlessly, moving from place to place. If there was some pathology at play (or at work), it struck me as a solution more than a problem. "Episodes of sudden, unexpected and purposeful travel from home," in Merck's words. If "dissociative fugue" was flight *away from*, this felt more like flight *toward* some ever-receding horizon. I felt no guilt; I was, after all, subsidizing my travels with my writing. I wasn't needed anywhere at present, as far as I could see—my father laid to rest, Masako deep in her own work, my adult daughter busy with her life. My wanderlust had picked up a momentum I couldn't seem to arrest, and I didn't care.

In my restless fiesta, there was little I missed. Each trip provided its own sustenance: borne by car, plane, bus, or taxi to the Hotel California, the Xibalbá in Palenque, Edward James's El Castillo, Hacienda Katanchel in the Yucatán, I'd encountered such companionship as I required—Jeanine from my past in the Sierra Gorda, Eduardo the film maniac in Mexico City, Gustavo Servin in Xalapa, David and crew in Palenque. Cities and villages, rivers and ruins: I'd entered a realm of endless invitation. I felt perfectly dissociated, outrunning time itself, with all the innocence of an amnesiac. The fact that I could no longer identify solid ground behind me, while I was chewing up ground beneath me, provided not panic but release. Why wasn't everybody doing what I was doing? Contemporary people carry plastic cards in their pockets enabling them to take off anywhere, anytime; yet inexplicably, so few do. That night, stepping off the bus in misty Xalapa, I could only think of the Greek poet C. P. Cavafy's lines, in which he counsels Homer's Odysseus:

When you set out on your journey to Ithaca
then pray that the road is long . . .

The taxi ride through drizzle reprised the earlier arrival, unfolding a Xalapa I knew a little now and had an affection for: along Xalapeños Ilustres, past the street called Primo Verdad and the turnoff to the Hotel California, down steep Calle Sebastián Camacho to the iron gate. As I hauled my bags up the stairs beside the main house, the mist suddenly cleared, in that shape-shifting way of Xalapa weather, revealing a fat, full moon above. I heard music playing somewhere. Exultant to be back, eager to taste silence and solitude again, I turned the corner to the little yellow house.

Gustavo Servin and a crowd of people were standing in the ruined garden, laughing and talking beneath paper lanterns. There were tables of food and drink. Sade's "Smooth Operator" wafted from a portable CD player.

"*¡Qué milagro! ¡Bienvenido!* Welcome back!" Gustavo called, rushing forward to enfold me in an abrazo. "It's my birthday. We're having a little fiesta. Put your bags down and come join us."

"*Sí, gracias,*" I murmured.

I opened the casita door, flicked on a light, and set down my bags. The little yellow house looked as I'd left it but for dust, a few cucaracha corpses, and the faint aroma of mold. I opened the shutters over the desk: the view to the volcano Citlaltépetl was now interrupted by party lanterns.

No chance of sleep for a while, let alone rest. Mexican sociability, to a visitor from the privacy-obsessed Protestant north, has its strained moments. The fact that I paid rent, however modest, for this place might have dissuaded a U.S. or European landlord from having a party in my garden. But when you've grown up in a swarming Catholic household, what's a little noise and proximity among friends? To put on a sour face would be further evidence of the tight, unflowing mien North Americans are often accused of bearing. If I'd found many habits in Mexico easy to adapt to, even preferable to our own ways, brushing aside the sense of personal invasion was one of the hardest for a gringo, even after years at it. With little choice but to join the fiesta in progress, I walked outside into Gustavo Servin's birthday party.

Servin introduced me around. "This is Marisela, an architect who teaches with me at the university. She made the *mole*. Juan Carlos, who has a great new restaurant."

"*Hola. Mucho gusto.*"

"*Encantado.*"

There was a young artist named Alicia, who seemed to be Servin's girlfriend; Ignacio, a surgeon at La Salud Hospital; Ofélia, an "actress and midwife"; and her husband Martín, a sculptor who spoke French to his son. All of them seemed curious as to why I was in Xalapa. "The weather," I tried to jest, which invariably elicited the term *chipichipi* in response.

Servin's garden party could have been in San Francisco or Chapel Hill or Austin, Paris or Prague or Buenos Aires. At a certain level of education and economic life, global culture had become generic. Pasta salad, French bread, chicken with mole sauce, guacamole. Beer, tequila, wine. Mostly American and British pop. Even the rebozo draped around the shoulders of the Mexican actress/midwife could have been seen at a party in Berkeley or Tokyo. Servin's friends were the cool, professional, artistic people of Xalapa.

"*Es una porquería. No ha hecho nada.*" It's a sham. He hasn't done anything.

The bearded journalist offering his critique of new president Vicente Fox's early performance now turned toward me expectantly. I steeled myself for what felt like the run-up to a political question. Recent events had cast me—every American abroad—into the grotesque, insupportable role of personal explicator of the actions of George W. Bush. For a moment I thought: *I can't handle this tonight, not after my Mexican bus ride.* I was about to say something like "If you think Vicente Fox is bad . . ." when the *chipichipi* returned, as quickly as it had dispersed—a blast of *frío*, fog and drizzle, turning us into soggy ghosts, shifting the conversation and rescuing me.

I bid my goodnights, wished Servin another happy birthday, and turned to head for my casita.

"*Oye*, Tony," Servin called after me. "There's something I need to talk to you about. I'll be in Mexico City for a couple of days. When I get back, we talk, okay?"

"Okay."

The garden fiesta continued a little while longer until the drizzle became a shower. The last thing I remember before sleep finished me off was Whitney Houston's umpteenth repeat of "I Will Always Love You" abruptly aborting, leaving only the kinder music of Xalapa rain on my roof.

The next morning rain had wiped the sky clean. I stood in the middle of a bright green bowl of high tropical valley. Out the window above the writing desk, beyond the paper lanterns and soggy party equipment, hawks and *zipolotes* banked against a hard cobalt sky, then glided across the mountain face in silvery light. The grand, snowy volcano was there to greet me.

So was mold—green, dank, dusty fungus that in my absence had invaded clothes, bedding, towels, and sheets. It had sprouted in the *canastas* where I'd left clothes, the unpacked suitcase, the suitcase itself. Green lichen crept up the base of the interior white walls. Little in the casita had escaped Xalapa's relentless damp.

I took the clothes and bedding out into the old garden, spread them along the wall ledge in the sun, and began beating them with a broom handle, choking among clouds of green dust. If this didn't work, I'd have to buy new clothes and blankets. Here, I thought, was the underside of chipichipi.

Back inside I emptied my shoulder bag of travel stubs and receipts, notebooks and papers. I spread out my writing things at the desk. Then, as a hotplate severely narrows the culinary options, I jotted down a few elemental provisions: eggs, chorizo, chiles, pasta, tortillas, onions, garlic, milk, yogurt. Locking the casita door behind me, I took the slippery brick path down to the street and hiked up Sebastián Camacho to the centro.

At Café La Parroquia, where Servin had first introduced me to the lechera, I sat among clattering dishes, clouds of smoke, heavy-lidded intellectuals in stained jackets bent over tomes, and valise-toting businessmen plotting the day's moves. A waiter in a white jacket streamed hot milk from a metal pitcher into my glass of black coffee, giving teeth to the word *infusion*—not unlike the mint tea ritual in a Moroccan café. The effects of a second lechero sent me bounding onward to the open coffee counter at Café Colón on Primo Verdad where, clothed in the scent of the bean that sustained the region, I bought a kilo of a dark blend for the house's little espresso maker.

After gathering the foods on my list at local markets, I dropped into a cybercafé full of hunkered game-playing kids who looked like they'd slept in their clothes. There was a bright e-mail from Masako in Oaxaca—more art, fiestas, another eclectic gathering at Laura Hernández's house. The following week she planned to return to San Miguel. What were my thoughts, my plans? A brief, memo-style query from the maga-zine editor asked how the piece was coming.

And there was one from Lauren.

Querido Antonio,

Imagine this as handwritten, on real paper, a few weeks old, slightly crumpled, delivered by some friend who carried it down in her handbag and just happened to be passing through. Like in the old days.

 I think of you often, and of Mexico, of course. Wondering where this may find you is its own diversion. Palenque? The Yucatán? La capital? Back home in San Miguel? I hope your wanderlust is treating you tenderly. That last night together at Ambos Mundos was almost too much, no? Híjole . . .

 What was that "fugue" term you used that night? Why must travel be described as an affliction? Of course it's an affliction, the best kind.

 Here at Ground Zero, we survive, slightly crumpled. I'll stay here a little longer until Celia is restabilized, which is to say soon. Then I will choose among a sublet in the West Village, an invitation from a friend in Montclair, another in Sag Harbor. Plans A, B, and C.

 Brutal times, my friend. I try to avert eyes and ears from the public spectacle. But it's all there is, it seems. Here, people seem to confuse information with experience.

 Still, an odd cheer besets the city, bound in adversity. Full of Mexicans these days too. They hover outside of the markets waiting for work . . .

 An old friend, an editor, has given me a good Spanish novel to translate. Mostly I stand at Celia's repaired

*window, looking at sky and holes in the ground, NPR on
in the background.*

*Was it a good idea to come back? Well, it wasn't an
idea, it was a response.*

*I feel trapped here inside the castle walls. When you
get back to San Miguel, or wherever you settle out for a
while, loft news over the moat.*

*What do I miss? Tacos al carbon at midnight from
the little puesto on Zacateros. Walking through the deserted jardín in early morning. Bearing home an armload
of fresh alcatrastes from the mercado and arraying them
in my Dolores Hidalgo vase by the window with the view
of Las Monjas. The bells, the bells, the consoling bells . . .*

Celia sends an abrazo. That makes two from here.

> *Yours, slightly crumpled,*
>
> *Lauren*

Before logging off, I sent my quick, fateful note to my
friend Sacha telling him I'd found the perfect honeymoon spot
for him and his new bride—Hacienda Katanchel in the Yucatán.
No es un hotel, I wrote ringingly, *es un sueño.*

For the next several days I stayed in the casita and wrote.
In what passed for a kitchen, I worked up a chorizo omelet with
fresh tortillas and salsa, accompanied by the universal Mexican
bread roll, the *bolillo*, and the beer called Indio. Evenings I wan-

dered the misty city, up the old walkstreet called Calle Diamante among the hippie sellers of jewelry and incense, or in one
of the city's countless cafés among intense, tobacco-stung read-
ers of books and willowy young students.

Back at the yellow house, morning sun and successive
beatings had rescued most of the bedding, and some socks and
shirts, from the green powdery mold, but not two pairs of shoes,
pants, and a suitcase. No word yet from Servin.

Each morning I walked out into the creeper-clogged garden, a mug of Xalapa coffee in hand, lowered myself into a sagging chair, and saluted snow-ringed Citlaltéptl. Then invoking
the shade of Malcolm Lowry—who, after writing perhaps the
best Mexican gringo novel, *Under the Volcano*, had died stupe-
fied on drink and pills in an English cottage—I arrayed the journeys of recent months about me like so much footage and set
to work.

I wrote about the high mountain idyll of the Sierra
Gorda—its lazy rivers and tropical valleys, Franciscan missions
and surreal jungle gardens; Mexico City's intensity and cultural
turmoil; efflorescent Oaxaca and the guiding figure of Francisco
Toledo; Guanajuato's twisting, tunneled dreamscapes, its
phantoms and ghosts. I wrote of Veracruz State: Xalapa, with
its coffee and orchids and mists; sweet Tlacotalpan's wide river
and pastel buildings and son jarocho pulse. I wrote of the
Mayan regions I'd visited: languid Mérida, the jungle retreat
of Katanchel, Palenque's singing ruins, the weaving women of
Chiapas.

I knew that had I chosen different voyages, I could have

written any number of parallel pieces equally representative of Mexico today. I'd left out the country's thousands of miles of coastline, with its villages, towns, resorts, and empty beaches— Pacific Zihuatanejo, Acapulco, Puerto Escondido, Puerto Ángel, Juchitán, Mazatlán; the Atlantic's Veracruz City, Cancún, Tulum, all the way south to Belize. Mexico City alone, for all its problems, was an inexhaustible subject, especially in these resurgent days. The vibrant north—Chihuahua, Monterrey, the Copper Canyon, Baja California—presented an entirely different Mexican face. Life along the vast border region, *la frontera* itself, surely represented Mexico today as much as anywhere I'd visited. The more I looked, the more Mexico appeared fathomless. Yet as Francisco Toledo was showing us in Oaxaca, it was impossible, maybe meaningless, to separate Mexico today from Mexico yesterday: it was upon the stones of Monte Albán, not the shopping mall and the parking structure, that a meaningful Mexican present would be found, a future built.

On the third afternoon, in need of a break, I took a taxi ride to Coatepec, twenty minutes away. The little town, whose very name is synonymous with coffee, gathers around a leafy plaza with an art nouveau bandstand, then spreads down wide, straight streets past orchid groves and balconied mansions echoing the wealth the *cafeteros* had brought Coatepec a century earlier—as silver had to Guanajuato, henequen to the Yucatán. Not far beyond Coatepec, in humid palm jungle, I came to the quiet, half-deserted mountain village of Xico, where horsemen rode cobbled streets past graceful colonial buildings and a sprawling parish church. Another beautiful old town, still in endless supply in Mexico. *What would it be like to live here?* I wondered, as I had so many times on my journeys. Artists had begun moving to Xico as they had to San Miguel fifty years ago, little galleries and gift shops sprouting to lure weekenders from Xalapa.

I hiked a road below Xico that cut through coffee and banana plantations, bringing me to a lookout over the tall forest waterfall of Texolo. Watching naked brown kids splashing in the pool beneath the cascade, I realized I'd barely touched upon this region in my travels. Veracruz City's carnival revels would soon draw people from all over Mexico and beyond. I'd yet to visit the coastal ruins of Tajin north of here, the town of Papantla with its flying acrobats, the countless interior villages that friends had insisted I must see. Even their names bewitched: Tuxpan, Tamiahua, Chicontepec, Coatzacoalcos. There were Veracruz's other great cities—Córdoba, Fortín de las Flores, Orizaba—and farther south, beyond Tlacotalpan, the cities of the Tuxtla, and lakeside Catemaco where witches and healers convened. Standing by the Texolo waterfall, spume spray cooling my face, I felt I was just beginning some endless Mexican journey.

I took a rickety local bus back to Xalapa, sitting on a hard metal seat among campesinos, a bottle of Xico liqueur and a jiggling plastic bag of *mole* in my lap, the driver singing to the radio's *música tropical*. Back in the city I bought a roasted chicken dripping on a spit, with red rice and salsa, to take back to the casita. Waiting for the man to wrap it, I thought of Lauren in Manhattan, standing at the plate-glass window of her daughter's apartment, and her comment that in my country information so often gets mistaken for experience. Flush with my sense-driven trip to Coatepec and Xico, bearing my aromatic chicken home through the Xalapa twilight to the little yellow house, I thought, No, experience is information you can count on.

That night and the following day I wrote about ghosts and dreams, and people who were no longer here or never had been: Frida, Huston, Buñuel; Raúl Hellmer the gringo jarocho; Guanajuato's Fitzcarraldo and Don Quixote and Dr. Leroy; Junípero Serra and Edward James; the ancient Mexica and Maya and Olmec and Zapotec. I wrote of inns and hotels, restaurants and markets and food stalls; of Oaxacan *mole*, Veracruz lecheros, Mayan *puuc chuc*. I wrote of not-so-distant neighbors in Guanajuato's Barrio Nuevo and their harrowing passages to Los Estados; idealistic Aníbal González in Katanchel, whose quixotic dream would soon be measured by nature; the artist Laura Hernández and the photographer Antonio Turock in Oaxaca. I recalled the demonstrations I'd seen in so many towns, eruptions of concern and conscience, objection and outrage against the U.S. response to 9/11.

Writing this, I felt far from the magazine editor's concerns. I'd experienced far more than any single piece could possibly include. Perhaps she could use a portion of this. If not, *ni modo.*

The next morning I began writing about San Miguel de Allende, the town I knew beneath its patina of movie productions and tourism. As I did, I began to miss the house on Calle Flor, the jardín, places and spaces as intimate as the lines in my palm, the community of souls I'd lived among for so long. I missed Masako, too, and what we'd made there and found in ourselves. Summoning things I loved, I began loving them again, writing my way back to where I once belonged.

Though I couldn't see it yet, this was the first rupture in my fugue.

Late that morning I heard voices outside. Looking up from the desk, I saw two men standing in the garden. One was old and thin, in a worn, shiny suit, smoking a cigarette. The other was ruddy, younger, in a loud shirt and cream-colored slacks. How had they gotten onto the locked property? I walked outside and greeted them. The older one stepped forth, offering his hand.

"Emilio Servin Alvárez, *a sus órdenes*," he said. "I am Gustavo's uncle. The *dueño*, the owner, of this property. And this is Señor Gómez Moreno, the man I am selling it to. I've come from Mexico City to finalize arrangements."

"Gustavo hadn't said anything about this."

"No? Ah, well, don't worry. Any friend of Gustavo's is a friend of mine."

The uncle had a pencil mustache and thinning, badly dyed hair. A cigarette dangled from stained, quivering fingers. He reminded me of those old gents I used to see at the Café La Blanca in downtown Mexico City.

"Take your time," he said. "If you need some days, that's

fine. A week even. No rush. It's just that Señor Gómez here wants to get started."

Señor Gómez said, brightly, "Condominiums." His sweeping arm took in the valley and the volcano. "With this view . . ."

They continued their stroll around the property, chatting and gesturing. A locksmith arrived and began changing the padlocks on the doors and gates.

"But how can I get in and out?" I asked Emilio Servin.

"No te preoccupes," he said. "I'll give you the new keys."

"Do you mind if I call Gustavo?" I said.

"Of course not. He's a fine young fellow. Give him my saludos."

I called Servin's mobile from inside the casita but only got his recorded voice. I left a message telling him to call me immediately.

After giving me new keys to house and gate, Gustavo's uncle and Señor Gómez left. I stood numbly in the garden, watching the daily haze roll in until it obscured the mountain and the city below. Clearly I was in the middle of some family property dispute.

I went back to the desk but couldn't concentrate. I felt as if the chair had been snatched out from under me. I lay on the bed, staring at the ceiling. It was always such a struggle, starting up with writing. I'd just gotten into a flow; now I'd broken stride. I could feel it. For all my rantings about endless travel, I realized ruefully that when it came time to write, I needed to park myself somewhere.

I thought of moving back to the Hotel California. But that sounded eerie, fatal, playing into the song's ominous message: you can check out anytime you like, but you can never leave.

Late that afternoon Servin called back. "I just got back from Mexico City. What's up?"

"Your uncle was here with a man he says he's selling this property to. They changed all the locks. They want me out."

"Damn!" he said. "That's what I wanted to talk to you about. It's my crazy uncle Emilio from Mexico City. Don't believe a word he says. Why didn't you call me?"

"I did."

"Okay. I'll be right over. Everything will be fine. *No te preoccupes*."

Half an hour later Servin and I stood in the garden, watching another locksmith cut the locks and install a new set.

"I was afraid he might do this," Gustavo said. "Uncle Emilio has no right. My father left this property to me. I'm going to put out a *demanda* on him in the morning." Gustavo handed me my new keys. "You can stay as long as you want. Take my word for it. Come on, let's go have a drink."

Closing the gate behind us, I wondered if I'd return later to find yet another new set of locks barring my entry.

"Did you tell my uncle you're paying me rent?" Servin asked as we walked into town.

"No."

"Okay, good."

The drink devolved into a dinner of pepper steak, *filete pimiento*, at the new restaurant of Servin's friend Juan Carlos, whom I'd met at the rainy birthday party in the garden. It was set in a shady grove across from the university among huge aurucaria trees, palms and orchids, with white walls and tablecloths, waiters dressed in black, Cesaria Evora playing in the background. There were few customers, and Juan Carlos was nowhere to be seen. Servin said it was the lunchtime comida crowd that supported the place.

He talked about his new girlfriend in Mexico City and the architecture department at the university. He talked about the traffic problem in Xalapa—anything but what had happened that afternoon with the house and his uncle. Finally, over flan and coffee, I brought it up.

"But is the property his or yours?"

Gloom suffused Servin's face. "Uncle Emilio is a *ladrón*, a thief. He sponged off my father for years. Nobody in the family will talk to him. Now he's claiming this place is his."

I couldn't get a straight answer. It was a familiar Mexican exercise: loose edges, fluid time, nothing pinned down. Things would work themselves out, or they wouldn't; inevitably there would be waiting involved, most likely an equivocal result, and everyone could claim machismo had been preserved. *No te pre-occupes.* I smelled the inception of a morass.

"The casita is yours. If Uncle Emilio shows up again, call me immediately. He's not allowed to do what he did today."

I figured I could probably stay on a while, never knowing quite when I'd arrive home to find the locks changed again, possibly permanently, my stuff trapped inside. In moments like these, I felt very much the foreigner. Napoleonic law, the general imprecision of Mexican civic life, seldom came to the gringo's aid in these situations.

We finished the meal laughing about something, our spirits lifted in spite. Gustavo was so likable, so sincere, it was hard to hold him to account for the confusion about the casita. We walked back through a clear, quiet night, free of Xalapa's purgatorial chipichipi, and parted at the corner of Xalapeños Ilustres.

To my relief, the keys opened the gate and the casita door. But climbing into bed, I thought: *No, this won't work anymore.* My days in the casita were numbered. The writing line had broken. With it, wanderlust's infinite horizon line had begun to contract.

Two mornings later, in a soft mist, I packed my books, my pages, and such possessions as had survived the mold, and boarded a bus back to San Miguel.

Three

"*What was mere romance to us has now become real memory.*"

—V. S. PRITCHETT

18.

Fugue

On February 27, 2003, almost one year to the day after I left Xalapa, I took an early afternoon direct bus from Querétaro, a city an hour from San Miguel, to the Mexico City airport, a journey of three hours. My plane to Bolivia was to leave at seven-thirty that evening. I was the only passenger in the line at the Lloyd Aereo Boliviano window, allowing for a quick check-in of the backpack I planned to live out of for the month-long trip, though the absence of other flyers was disconcerting.

I shouldn't have been surprised. When I'd come across the Lloyd Aereo Boliviano flight on the Net, I'd leaped at the incredibly cheap fare. It was only after I'd purchased my ticket that a savvy traveler friend told me that a string of mishaps and near-mishaps around South America had all but grounded the airline, leaving it teetering on the edge of suspension and insolvency. Now a pariah among carriers, with one of the worst safety records in the skies, Lloyd Aereo Boliviano was practically giving tickets away.

Walking toward the departures area, I suddenly got cold feet. I wasn't sure I wanted to go. This had been a trip I'd long planned: Bolivia, Peru, Chile. If living in Mexico had enriched my American self, this was the next increment. My Spanish was good now; inevitable that I'd reach out into greater Latin America. I'd write about the trip. I had many good reasons for going.

This wasn't the sort of self-convincing I'd had to do when my fugue was in full flower.

A year had passed since my return from Xalapa to San Miguel. Of the voyages around Mexico commissioned by the magazine, in the end the editor had built the story around Oaxaca—a fitting choice, as no single place more embodied what was "new and exciting" in Mexico these days. The piece included an interview I did with the artist Francisco Toledo in his L.A. exile; and a photographer sent to Oaxaca by the magazine managed to capture some of the visual excitement I'd found and written about, including the beautiful artist Laura Hernández.

The editor had been prescient about Mexico as a travel destination. As post-9/11 uncertainties steered wary travelers away from Europe and Asia, not to mention the Middle East, U.S. tourists clung to their hemisphere, coming to Mexico not just to visit but to live. Joining a host of new retirees, younger settlers, realizing they could manage their work through some combination of the Internet and commuting, brought families to Mexico to raise, enrolling their children in bilingual schools. Other North Americans, disenchanted with the country's political direction, lit out across the border, as in earlier epochs. Meanwhile the flow northward continued unabated, Mexico's new government unable to provide any more jobs for its people than its predecessors.

In San Miguel, already weathering the onslaught of gentrification, the new wave hit, sending prices skyward, filling restaurants and bars and hotels, stocking the jardín with more gringos. Buyers flew down from San Francisco or New York for the weekend to snap up houses for shocking figures. Eateries raised prices and reprinted their menus with English above the Spanish, causing Xavier to grouse, "I'm thinking of teaching classes in Spanish as a second language for Mexicans." El Vigilante, whose paranoid letters excoriating the foreign presence had gotten him run out of town, would have been scribbling even more furious diatribes were he still around.

Shiatsu, yoga, Pilates, spas, face-lift clinics. San Miguel was awash in a riot of New Age (or "newage"—as in "sewage," a friend darkly joked), ever more resembling places the new settlers had fled. Supply stores located around the jardín, no longer able to afford the rent, ceded their quarters to boutiques or gift shops and migrated to the outskirts. Traffic backed up along San Miguel's old narrow streets. Many Mexicans, even those benefiting from the boom, felt pushed around, openly airing their complaints on Radio XESQ. "People used to worry San Miguel was going to become the next Santa Fe," I heard an old-timer say one night at the Ambos Mundos. "We're way past that. Welcome to the new Florida." Xavier commented mordantly that he longed for the good old days of *Once Upon A Time in Mexico*. "At least Salma and Johnny and Banderas were nice to look at," he said. A gringo who had run an ice cream store as a front for selling black market goods and investing other foreigners' savings for them had died suddenly, slumped over his computer, leaving a trail of blown investments worth millions—unrecoupable, it was becoming clear, as his Mexican widow, who ran a chicken store on Calle Mesones, claimed to have known nothing about any of it.

Trouble in paradise. A Californian, I knew its symptoms well. But none of it diminished the sweet air, the shimmering light, the bougainvillea-splashed courtyards, the soft evenings and tolling bells, the perfect feng shui of San Miguel's hillside setting. The purple jacarandas exploded early that spring, and the fiestas and parades and celebrations furnished their cacophony of splendors as ever. Devout parishioners filled La Parroquia for mass every night, ardent voices raised heavenward. The *alegría*, *sabor*, and *ambiente* that had always drawn people to the little mountain town remained undimmed. And up in Colonia Azteca, Hilario's once-humble neighborhood, the run-up in prices would make the gardener a rich man one day.

After all, wasn't it the same everywhere with the last good places? Cranky veterans could console themselves with goat cheese and brie, *caffè latte*, concerts and readings, the film series at the *biblioteca*'s new theater. And at night at El Petit Bar, or down at the venerable La Cucaracha in the wee hours, remnants of San Miguel's old bohemia could creep out of their niches to revel and rail.

Along Calle Flor life was little different but for more cars on the street and the neighbors' new wall blocking sunlight into our rear garden. Masako arrived back from Oaxaca soon after I returned, her beautiful book on Mexican textiles done at last. The vivid world we'd knitted together behind high rose walls, and the sustaining town beyond, muted our restlessness, our questionings, the alarming drift in the greater world. Masako had several art shows upcoming, including the one at Francisco Toledo's gallery in Oaxaca, and needed to get to work in her studio off the rear garden. A tall, narrow, onetime stable with crumbling asbestos laminate roofing and slumping adobe walls, it didn't look as if it would last through the summer rains. Something had to be done.

The very word *remodel* charged the air between us. A decade earlier we'd built stone stairs and a rooftop veranda in the old finca, and by the end we were barely speaking. Epifánio, the maestro we'd worked with, still recovering from the car crash outside of town with his whores, was out of the question. We worked up a simple plan with a local architect; then with all that was uncertain and unsettled in us stirring in the wings, we went ahead. Soon after Semana Santa, Holy Week, the ringing of chisels could be heard out back.

To escape the noise, I'd sometimes walk to the Parque Juárez, where egrets nested in the tall trees and sheltered gardens afforded refuge. One day there I ran into Juan José and Beatriz—Lupe's kids, whose wedding I'd attended the fall be-

fore at San Francisco Church—bearing their new little swaddled girl, Caterina. Juan José was busy at his ironmonger's job;
and to the family's relief, his troubled sister Juanita had broken
up with Chuy, her gangster boyfriend, and returned home. This
meant Lupe had a full house and then some, with no relief in
sight.

It was a hot, dry April, and I was starting to miss Xalapa's
cool mists when an e-mail came from Gustavo Servin. The yellow casita was still there empty, the property locked in litigation
with the weird uncle from Mexico City. "So you see?" Servin
wrote, unconvincingly. "You could have stayed on."

Early that summer the Day of the Locos parade visited its
annual madness on the town, wilder and more maniacal than
ever. Thousands danced through the streets in masks and costumes and outlandish drag, a medieval Saint Vitus' dance, as if
to exorcise demons of war and discontent. Bobbing alongside
the usual hookers and goblins, devils and priests, transvestites
and wobbly giants came rubbery, jug-eared George Bush
masks, eerily resembling Alfred E. Neuman, outnumbering the
Saddams, a favorite of years past, and even the mustachioed,
long-faced Presidente Foxes.

By July the studio renovation had lurched to its niggling
end of scrap and finish detail. The last workers cleared out, returning us to our silence, our work, and our pleasures along
Calle Flor. Then deep summer's sweet spot arrived, cloaking us
all in golden light. Long, warm days and nights cooled by rains.
Smell of hot roasting corn, fireworks, and *globos* lighting up the

fairyland night skies. Faces we hadn't seen in years—young ones dandling new babies, older ones grandchildren—appeared in the jardín and along the *calles*. The bars thrummed with music, people spilled out into the streets, the stars came down so close they almost broke in our eyes. Everything was young again, everyone was in love with somebody or something, everyone was immortal. *¡México querido y lindo!*

Still, sometimes I'd recall Lauren's words over dinner that night at the Ambos Mundos—about wanting to be at the center or at the edges, not in some globalized expatriate limbo. As September's patriotic festivities loomed, my gaze turned southward, to that other hemisphere. I read Neruda and Mistral, Cortázar and Borges, Chatwin and Theroux. I read a biography of Che Guevara that Eduardo had thrust upon me in Mexico City, and Che's own *Motorcycle Diaries*. Studying maps of Bolivia, Peru, Chile. Staring at the dwindling bottom of the continent, the ends of the earth: Punta Arenas, Tierra del Fuego, Ushuaia. Sketching out a voyage.

"Most fugues," Merck had said, "end on their own."

All year long I'd had intimations that my travel compulsion was abating. But I hadn't regained the art of sitting still either. There seemed to be no escape from escape.

To rid myself of my fugue, I would have to make a journey into travel itself.

During that fall's alarming run-up to the invasion of Iraq, I sometimes tried to puzzle out a connection between my lingering restlessness and these new shadows stalking the earth, but

I found no simple answer. As the year wound down, Masako readied to return to the little place in Oaxaca she'd rented to prepare for her show there. I began researching flights.

I'd planned to travel around Bolivia first, beginning in the capital, La Paz, as it was the country I suspected would interest me most. Then a month before my departure, thirty-three Bolivian protesters were shot and killed in La Paz's Plaza de Armas, in front of the capitol building, a block from the hotel where I'd be staying. Army and police had attacked the protesters and each other. There were demonstrations and roadblocks throughout the country. The indigenous *cocalero* union was protesting the U.S.-backed government of Sánchez Lozano, described in the media as a "Texas-bred filmmaker." U.S. State Department travel advisories warned citizens against entering the country.

I took the advisories with a measure of skepticism. Among travelers on the ground, U.S. travel advisories had little credibility and were often made fun of. In Mexico they often appeared after some random assault on a tourist in a remote Guerrero stretch of beach, or as a punitive response to some contretemps between Washington and the Mexican government. Sometimes the safest place to be was exactly where the State Department warned you not to go. You just needed to know your way around, take the normal precautions. The advisory gave big play to a report that some months earlier a European couple had been attacked by a local mob in southern Bolivia, triggered by rumors Europeans were seeking babies for their body parts.

Bolivia, I knew, had had more changes of government than any country on earth, the average regime lasting a year and a half. But if strikes or roadblocks prevented my traveling by road within the country, they would hobble my plans: after La Paz I'd planned to go to Cochabamba and Sucre in the south, then to Copacabana and Titicaca in the north, entering Peru from there. I decided to make the trip anyway, but in reverse, beginning in Chile, delaying my entry into Bolivia until last, in the hope that things would have calmed down. The plane would fly to Santa Cruz, a hub airport in southern Bolivia, where I'd change planes and fly over the Andes to Santiago, the capital of Chile.

With the turning of the new year, Masako and I found ourselves saying goodbye again. "How can I miss you if you won't go away?" The old song by Dan Hicks and his Hot Licks had always made us laugh in recognition. Still not wanting to confuse distance with rupture, breaks with endings. Still trusting in the process of separation to guide us to where we were supposed to be.

I was crossing the Mexico City departures terminal to the Lloyd Aereo Boliviano gate when I saw Lauren, coming off a Delta flight from New York. Tall and dramatic, with her long dark hair and her shawl, striding off the ramp, unmistakably herself. I couldn't have been more surprised.

"Lauren!"

She turned, confused, then spotted me.

"*¡Qué milagro!*" I said as we embraced.

"You bet," she said, laughing. "Where are you off to now?"

"South America."

"Still in your wanderlust."

"On its last legs, I think. How's Celia?"

"Fine. Just fine. Back in classes at NYU."

"What about you?"

"I'm here. I'm standing."

"Where are you headed?"

"Where do you think?"

"For a visit?"

She shook her head and grinned.

"You've come back."

Lauren shrugged her tall shoulders. "If your heart isn't happy," she said, her eyes filling with tears, "then what's the point?"

"*Bienvenida,*" I said. It was very good news.

"How long will you be gone?"

"A month." I heard my flight being called.

"I'll meet you at La Ventana on Calle Sollano for a *café con leche,*" she said. "In a month."

"I'll be there."

"I know you will."

As I turned to go, Lauren said, "Wait." She reached into her purse and pulled out an envelope. "Something to read on the plane."

The scant few of us gathered at the Lloyd Aereo Boliviano departure gate were summoned by loudspeaker to a shuttle bus and driven through foggy drizzle to a remote corner of the landing field. Few of my fellow passenger looked to be tourists. Some were short, dark Indians, Bolivian Aymara or Quiche perhaps, reminding me a little of Oaxaca's Zapotecs; others, to judge by their garb and mien, looked to be middle-class businessmen, Mexican or South American. There were a few families with babies wrapped in rebozos or shawls. A shabby little klatch of passengers we were. But what was to dress up for when we were going to spend all night in flight to the poorest country in South America?

The plane loomed ahead in the mist, a huge Boeing 747 of uncertain vintage, parked alone beside a chain-link fence at the farthest reaches of the airport, beyond the arc lights—as if Lufthansa and American Airlines and British Airways passengers were not to know that this flight took off from here at all. Hurrying across the airstrip in the rainy darkness, I felt as if I were boarding some remote Aeroflot flight in 1950s Tajikistan, or I'd blundered into *Casablanca*'s final scene with Bogie and Claude Rains.

I climbed on board and found my way to my seat. Oddly, they'd grouped the several dozen of us into one corner of the gigantic plane, along one side, near the front of economy class, leaving the rest of the plane, center and right, fore and aft, virtually empty. Was this good for the weight distribution? Of course as soon as the seatbelt signs went off, everyone would migrate across the ocean of unoccupied seats and settle where they could stretch out and sleep. For now, I was sandwiched in between a corpulent, heavy-breathing man who looked to be

European and smelled of drink, and an indigenous woman with her sleeping baby swaddled in a colored shawl. Suddenly the idea that tiny, poor Bolivia would even have an intercontinental airline seemed preposterous, suspect.

Riffling through the in-flight magazine while we waited for takeoff, I read a long editorial by the new president of Lloyd Aereo Boliviano, a man with a German last name, offering, in effect, a mea culpa for Lloyd's shaky flying record without actually owning up to it. He promised a better, safer airlines, a *"nuevo Lloyd Aereo Boliviano,"* as he put it, with planned nonstop service between Bolivia and Los Angeles.

When the plane's engines started up, passengers unwilling to wait until we were airborne began flooding the other sections of the plane. I joined the revolt and scrambled across the aisle to an empty middle row, a few seats behind the partition separating us from the deserted first-class section, where I could stretch out for the night.

As the 747 taxied down the runway, rain pelting the windows, a sudden desolation swept me. What was I doing out here? Was there no exit from this endless corridor of travel?

I took out Lauren's envelope. Inside I found a poem by our departed *amigo*, the gentle San Miguel poet Fernando Maqueo.

REGALO
Te regalo este lugar, hermano.
Te regalo este pedazo de cielo
Para que vengas a mirar la luna
Y las estrellas

A traves de las ramas y las flores
Y las hojas de eucalipto
En este instante
De ningún tiempo,
Que también te regalo.

GIFT

I give you this place, brother.
I give you this piece of sky
So you can come and look at the moon
And the stars
Through the branches and the flowers
And the eucalyptus leaves
In this instant
Of no time
That I also give you.

I gazed at the fuzzy green screen above me displaying the flight map that would track our voyage. The little plane icon, poised on Mexico City, pointed due south. Curaçao, Iguazú, Antofagasta, Belo Horizonte. Names off childhood maps. We were flying to a different corner of the world! Then as the Lloyd Aereo Boliviano rose, shuddering, into the air, I felt the rush of anticipation, mixed with fear.

About the Author

Tony Cohan is the author of *On Mexican Time* and *Native State* (a *Los Angeles Times* Notable Book of the Year), and the novels *Opium* and *Canary* (a *New York Times* Notable Book of the Year). His articles, essays, and reviews have appeared in the *New York Times*, the *Washington Post*, the *Los Angeles Times*, *Condé Nast Traveler*, and *The Times* (London). He divides his time between Mexico and California.

4/06